Thank you and Carolyn
for reading this book.
& hope you find it
worth your time.

Lex Browney

The Last Soul
of
Witherspoon

Life in a
Kentucky Mountain
Settlement School

Alex Browning

BALBOA.
PRESS
A DIVISION OF HAY HOUSE

Balboa Press books may be ordered through booksellers or by contacting:

Balboa Press
A Division of Hay House
1663 Liberty Drive
Bloomington, IN 47403
www.balboapress.com
1-(877) 407-4847

Printed in the United States of America.

ISBN: 978-1-4525-7176-8 (sc)
ISBN: 978-1-4525-7178-2 (hc)
ISBN: 978-1-4525-7177-5 (e)

Library of Congress Control Number: 2013906007

Balboa Press rev. date: 4/9/2013

Please ignore the following quote:

"Never read a book through merely because you have begun it."

John Witherspoon

(1723-1794)

———————————————

For all my relatives, past, present, and future—
with apologies all around.

Contents

Foreword—A Man's Character Is His Fate

Once upon a time, three life-times before my own, two men lived and died in such a way as to shape my own life. In the lives they led, these two men could not have been more at odds with each other in almost everything they did or believed. Though they never met, their lives almost crossed several times during the Civil War. Had they met, the outcome would have been dire. It was only fate that prevented the meeting. One of these men left a legacy; the other left many off-spring.

When I say these men shaped my life, one might question if my being Scotch-Irish, and Presbyterian at that, might influence my thinking. That conclusion could be somewhat accurate. However, rather than leaning on predestination and John Calvin to explain what I have become and what I have made of my life, I prefer to charge everything off to fate—though not with the meaning of fate as we generally define the word. Fate in my life is better explained by the Greek philosopher Heraclitus, who first penned the idea that a "man's character is his fate." That is what these pages are all about—how these two men, E.O. Guerrant and Captain David Hogan and their followers and off-spring, influenced my character—my own, and as it turned out, many others.

A psychiatrist once asked me why I hated myself, which was startling to me at the time because it never occurred to me that I had such feelings. After much introspection and mulling over his question, I thought, "Well, maybe he might be right." Certainly then and since there have been plenty of times when I have wished I could be somebody else or be somewhere else; so maybe at times I have hated myself or at least my life's condition. While the psychiatrist's question still reverberates, I doubt seriously I could have been anybody else or be somewhere else in life other than where I am right now. For sure, I do not hate myself or anyone as I sit down to pen these pages. No words here are written for revenge or to reveal flaws in any other person's character. After all, other people I have known have had to deal with their own fates. Anyway, many are dead and cannot speak for themselves even if they wanted to do so.

My one hope for the willing reader is agreement that actions do have consequences, be they immediate or somewhere farther down life's moral road; for as we learn from Gestalt psychology, all our actions do surely contribute to the sum total of our character which in turn likely determines the fate that befalls us. Whatever that ends up being probably will be etched in some pithy statement on our grave yard markers. The several hundred students who endured my English classes already know that I am requesting that my personal epithet come from the poet Shelley, who wrote, "If Winter comes, can Spring be far behind?" A further hope is that the meaning of this line will shine through as one reads the history and incidents that follow.

My goal in putting together my recollections and research findings on Witherspoon College is to put into perspective lives much more significant than my own: the lives of people who gave of their time and their riches to help shape the character of every person who attended Witherspoon College, more widely known as Buckhorn. I beg the reader to forgive my overuse of the pronoun "I." These pages were not intended to be just narcissistic exercise. However, much written here had to come from my own memory and seems best relayed from the first person. Above that, in every case the selective memories recalled here are for the purpose of providing a historical accounting of Witherspoon College (Buckhorn), which is a more challenging task than just writing about me.

An underlying reason for these pages actually comes from a personal experience I had many years after my Buckhorn years ended. A person for whom I once worked engaged himself in actions that I felt violated public trust. I refused to be a part of the plan even though I knew it meant the end of a successful career of sixteen years for me. Not being at all happy with me, my superior said he had never met anyone whom he disliked more than me and that he simply could not understand why I could be so obstinate. My response to him was, "Well, had you attended Witherspoon College, you would understand completely."

In recording this work, many people deserve special mention. I take this opportunity to pay tribute to just three of them. These people through their kindness and character made positive contributions to my own. The first, Miss Mary Wilson of the Maysville Kentucky Presbyterian Church who though she had very little herself, found ways to provide material support to me while I was in high school and college. Included also is Jean Keen Wooton for her encouragement during some tough times while I was at Buckhorn and who did so because that is just the kind of person she is and without even knowing of my problems. And, finally, also is Dr. Margaret Patton, my professor at both Pikeville College and Morehead State University. Mrs. Patton provided material support, taught me how to rhumba and not be so socially awkward, and defended me "against all odds." If the psychiatrist was right that I did hate myself, Mrs. Patton helped me believe I did not need to do that.

Alex W. Browning

Acknowledgements

Appreciation is expressed to the following sources:

Debra Callahan and Helen Wykle of the Pine Mountain Settlement School. These staff members were very helpful to me in obtaining a copy of their brochure on Witherspoon College developed by Dr. Elmer Gabbard during the early years of his administration of the school.

The Hutchins Library of Berea College. Archived here are records and photographs of the Buckhorn Association from 1902-1960. Of special use were the yearly reports given by the directors of the Association. The staff at the Hutchins Library was very helpful to me as I waded through microfilm.

Jean Keen Wooton. Mrs. Wooton deserves credit for putting up with me in class. She also spent hours with me answering questions and giving me her personal history of Buckhorn. Digging out her mother's notes helped me nail down dates.

Bjorn Larsson. Bjorn took time from his own schedule to help me obtain pictures and information on The Munson Line, a business interest of Edward F. Geer, the person behind The Log Cathedral.

Mary Alice Browning Pare. Anyone interested in the history of the Bowman or Browning families should always check their facts with Mary. She has done all the hard work.

The Lexington Herald-Leader. The publisher and department heads were more than kind to dig out a photograph from their files for me to use that had been stored more than twenty years.

Charles Boggs, The Buckhorn Children's Foundation. My special thank you for your permission for me to quote from minutes and records of the Buckhorn Association stored at Berea College, photos from the 1936 brochure of Witherspoon College, and from on-line information from the website of the Buckhorn Children's Foundation.

References and Recommended Reading

Appreciation is expressed to the following sources:

Administrator. "Edelen Releases Examination of the Breathitt County Board of Education." October 14, 2012. Website: http://breathittonline.com/blog/2012/10/14

Albertson, Charles C. LIGHT ON THE HILLS. J. B. Lippincott Company, 1905.

> *Charles Albertson was a pastor of the Lafayette Avenue Presbyterian Church and one of the original signers of the Act to incorporate the Buckhorn Association. The library was named after him. The selected poems provide insight to the thinking of the founders of Witherspoon College. Weighty topics include Life and Death, Immortality, The Blessed Dead, Heaven, Resurrection, and Recognition.*

Davis, William C. and Meredith L. Swentor. BLUEGRASS CONFEDERATE. Louisiana State University Press. 1999.

Farr, Sidney Saylor. MY APPALACHIA. The University Press of Kentucky. 2007.

Fox, John, Jr. THE TRAIL OF THE LONESOME PINE. Buccaneer Books, Inc., 1908.

Dr. Gabbard referenced this book in one of his publications to draw interest to Buckhorn. The book helped stereotype mountain living and dialect. There is a personal connection to my family. Colonel Campbell Slemp of the 64th Virginia Military was one of the few members of that fighting group to escape capture by Union forces and internment at Camp Douglas. The character of Black Hawk was patterned after Colonel Slemp. The book was made into a movie in 1936 and is credited with the first use of Technicolor for outdoor shooting. The movie is available now on DVD.

Guerrant, Edward O. THE GALAX GATHERER: THE GOSPEL AMONG THE HIGHLANDERS. The University of Tennessee Press. 2005.

Not only are Guerrant's own words important, the introduction to the book by Mark Huddle was my first awareness of the controversy involving home missionaries.

Kastenbaum, Lawrence. THE POLITICAL GRAVEYARD. Website: http://politicalgraveyard.com/bio/gabaldon-gafney.html

LAWS OF THE STATE OF NEW YORK. J.B. Lyon Company, State Printers. 1916

Mahy, G. Gordon, Jr. MURDOCH OF BUCKHORN. The Parthenon Press. 1946.

As long as this book exists, Dr. Murdoch's work will be remembered.

McAllister, J. Gray and Grace Owings Guerrant. EDWARD O. GUERRANT: APOSTLE TO THE SOUTHERN HIGHLANDERS. Richmond Press, Inc., 1950.

Chapter XIII is entitled "The Story of Harvey S. Murdoch and the Beginning of the School, Hospital, Church and Homes for Children at Buckhorn, Kentucky."

McCauley, Deborah. APPALACHIAN MOUNTAIN RELIGION: A History. University of Illinois Press, 1995.

This book is excellent for understanding mountain religion and the effects of denominational missionary work.

Moore, James D. PICTORIAL HISTORY OF WITHERSPOON COLLEGE—A SETTLEMENT SCHOOL IN EASTERN KENTUCKY. The Buckhorn Alumni Association, Inc. 2006.

If a picture is worth a thousand words, this is the book of reference for Witherspoon College.

Nicholls, Lewis D. A MASTERFUL RETREAT. Avant Garde Publishing. 2006.

There is no better or more complete telling of the 7th Division's Retreat across Eastern Kentucky from the Cumberland Gap that lasted from September 17 through October 3, 1862. My great-great grandfather was a Union soldier in the retreat to avoid capture by Confederate forces.

Potter, Annette Family Genealogy. Website: http://yeapot. com/badtomsmith.html

Prescott, Sarah. "Melvil Dewey, the Father of Modern Librarianship, Was One Strange Guy." School Library Journal, 08/01/2001

Pritchett, C. B. "Camp Douglas Civil War Prison, Chicago." Website: http://www.ncgenweb.us/transylvania/home_html/Camp-Douglas-Civil-War-Prison

Shapiro, Henry D. APPALACHIA ON OUR MIND. The University of North Carolina Press. 1978

Tabler, Dave. "How Could He Be a Republican?" Website: http:www.appalachianhistory.net/2011/01/how-could-he-be-a-republican.html

Timm, Holly. "Keeping the Home Fires Burning: Civil War in Southeast Kentucky." Website: http://www.rootsweb.ancestry.com/seky/civilwar/homefire/index.html

Whisnant, David E. MODERNIZING THE MOUNTAINEER. The University of Tennessee Press. 1980

CHAPTER 1

The Trip from Hope Road

A brilliant sheen of anticipation blanketed Hope Road on an already bright day in May, 1952, when Preacher McClure, our mission pastor from Booneville, Kentucky pulled up at our house on the head of the holler on Long Shoal in his heavy duty station wagon.

Of our location, my father often said, "Boys, this is it. We'll be all right here."

In making this statement, Dad had to be uttering more of a prayer than dealing with reality; for to my knowledge, no one has ever prospered from living at the head of our holler. What my father meant was that this could be our last stand. He had already spent most of the money he had saved from working at the Kings Powder Company in Ohio during World War II, where the work was so dangerous those employed there were not sent to fight at the front. In fact, my earliest memories as a child are of standing in front of a window in our living room every day worrying whether Dad would come home and adding to my mother's concerns by saying, "I hope he doesn't get 'bwode up'." Once there was an explosion at the plant that blew out the windows of houses in South Lebanon, which was located five miles from the powder mill. Imagine our anxiety that day.

1

Although he was not saying it, my father was making note that our house was as far as anyone could go up the holler. Behind us was a mountain, and there was a mountain on each of our sides. The road to our house was mostly on creek bed, which meant when the water was high we could only get out by riding a horse or walking over the hill. And sometimes the creeks did rise. Once when Dad came home from "Court Day" where he had been trading horses, he brought home a clear light fool of an unbroken horse. Somehow the horse was accidentally startled which caused him to break free from where he had been tied. When we tried to catch him, he ran right by us and straight into the raging creek. That horse has never been seen again. With further regard to what my father said, had anyone actually tried to find us, it is for sure no one could have done so by any road signs; for there were none. The road did not get its name Hope until fifty years later. I am sure my uncle Ben was being sarcastic and not idyllic when he named it.

Preacher McClure, however, knew where we lived and how to get there. And he had business on this day; for he was to take me to visit Buckhorn, about twenty-five miles away—to visit the school. If things worked out, he was also going to help me make arrangements to attend boarding school there for my high school education. Prior to this trip to Buckhorn, one of the biggest thrills of my life was to play in a softball game Preacher McClure had arranged between some of us on Long Shoal and players from Cow Creek, which was another mission church under his care as a Presbyterian minister. The game had to be scheduled at Cow Creek because where we lived there was not enough level ground for a playing field. Nor did we have bats or balls. Mr. McClure did not feel sticks and gum balls, our usual equipment, were suitable for this big time event; so he got the real stuff from somewhere. When the game ended, the final score was something like 15-2 in favor of the home team. Those of us who played still felt like winners for just getting to make the trip. We had traveled probably fifteen miles to get to the Cow Creek ball field; by far the longest most of us had been away from our homes at the time. At least it certainly was for me. Since my family had moved back to Kentucky from Ohio when I was nine years old, I had never been out of the Long Shoal Holler except to trek across the hill to Coal Branch where my Granny Bowman lived.

To be totally accurate, there was one other exception: each year all Long Shoal school children and their parents boarded a flat-bed truck for the trip to Beattyville to attend the Lee County Fair. Lizzie Fox, who believed it was sinful to not have her hair covered, suffered months of remorse following one of those trips because the wind blew her hat off and away. At Beattyville, we joined schools from all the outlying communities to march up Main Street. At the end of the march, we competed in foot races, broad and high jump, and in reading and arithmetic. One year when I did not have money for the carnival rides, I sold the ribbons I had won in the contests to one of the carnival vendors. Almost immediately when I got on the Tilt-A-Whirl, the speed of the turns threw my money out of my hand to be found no more. That annual trip had been both exciting and disappointing for me, but it was nothing compared to the nervousness I felt about the trip I was to make this day.

As a faithful follower of Preacher McClure, I had great admiration for him. But he was in many ways prone to fantastic thinking. Sometimes his ideas could be a marvel. Once, for example, in conceiving perhaps his grandest scheme, he asked members of his congregation in Booneville to bring rocks from their fields and place them in a pile at the church. For weeks then, in addition to and sometimes instead of tithing, those attending church also brought as many rocks as they could carry. When the pile of rocks reached the prescribed amount, they were used to construct a new church that stands even today as a monument to all these efforts. This plan of Preacher helped to clear fields for plowing, and additionally resulted in a building that turned out to be architecturally unique.

Other plans of Preacher McClure did not always turn out so well. One year he announced to our congregation that he was going to bring in a battery-powered movie projector to show the film *King of Kings*. Since there was no electricity up our way, this would be the first time many local citizens had ever seen a moving picture show. Word spread like a sage grass fire for this amazing event; and for the service the next week everybody for miles around showed up to witness their first movie.

Granny Bowman, though, was a hold-out. She felt pictures of religious figures like Jesus were idolatrous. The only picture of Christ she ever allowed in her house was a free art print she got from me when I sold her a can of Cloverine salve for twenty-five cents. I earned enough money from this work to surprise her with a New Testament in large print. Using my best sales closing techniques, I persuaded Granny that she benefited in three ways: she got a can of good salve; a beautiful art print suitable for framing; and the book she loved to read and now could without eye strain. She bought my pitch and the salve and hung the picture on her living room wall, along with the one she had of her whole family. The photograph included her, my grandfather who died before I was born, and their eleven living children. As it turned out, Granny and I were both fooled by that art print. It was a picture of Jesus with a heart on his chest. We did not know it, but art of such sort is related to the Roman Catholic faith, a religion my Granny would never have approved, although we knew practically nothing about it. Our objection would have been having priests as intermediaries to God. Granny needed no intercessor; she had her own direct line to the Almighty.

As it turned out, Granny's refusal to go to church that day did not make any difference. Preacher McClure forgot to bring the batteries for the projector. He apologized, rescheduled the event, and proceeded to deliver a substitute sermon for which he was poorly prepared, a rather common occurrence, I am sad to say. Presbyterians firmly advocate the scripture verse of Matthew 6, which says "When you pray, go into your room; and when you have shut the door, pray to your Father who is in the secret place; and your Father who sees you in secret will reward you openly." Many of Mr. McClure's sermons might better have been delivered in that same room.

On the re-scheduled date, Preacher McClure did remember to bring the batteries. But because many sinners up our way evidently had too little faith, attendance was much lower. If Heaven holds us accountable for sins of omission, surely Preacher McClure's forgetfulness that day cost him many converts. Those who did not return for the next opportunity to see the movie probably have since suffered the fate of eternal damnation for not for converting—except for Granny, who I am sure was already "saved."

Martha Gabbard, a lady who lived over the hill from my family, kept the Long Shoal Church together on Sundays when Preacher McClure could not get there because of bad roads. Martha was familiar with both Buckhorn and Berea College where she herself had gone to school, and she had encouraged me to go to one of them. Knowing of no other schools myself, I was easily sold on her suggestion.

There had been one other opportunity a year or so earlier. Miss Violet Siebert, a summer volunteer to our church from Princeton University, had offered to adopt me when I was ten. She proposed to take me back with her to New Jersey. My parents, after listening to me go on for days about how this would help me get good schooling, finally left the decision to me. My mother suspected that when the time came for me to actually face leaving home, I might not be so eager to pack my bags. Her patience was rewarded. I told everybody I felt too responsible to my sister Mary Alice, six years younger than I, to take Miss Siebert up on her offer. In reality, I probably would have cashed Mary in for a dime. I had already exposed my true feelings when I was taken to the hospital to see her in the nursery. (She was the only child in our family not delivered at home and the only one to have a real birth certificate.) My parents, being somewhat egocentric and proud of their new addition to the family, were sure I would make the right choice; so they let me select any baby I wanted in the nursery to bring home. I complained all the way back to our house because I did not want the red head, my sister, but wanted instead the baby with the full head of black hair. Even today I am not totally sold on all the virtues pointed out to me for selecting Mary, but that road not taken with regard to going to Princeton narrowed my choices to either Buckhorn or Berea.

Martha had a lot of community power because she was the person in touch with the Maysville Presbyterian Church. For those who attended Sunday school faithfully during the year, Martha sent their names to Maysville; and parishioners there rewarded them with a gift at Christmas by drawing their names in a lottery. For most of us, this present was our biggest and best gift for Christmas. All year long, we prayed, in our secret rooms, that a rich family would draw our names in the lottery. Martha communicated with Miss Mary Wilson in Maysville about the drawing. Miss Mary knew the resources of those in her own church, and we felt she likely could be influential as to which gift providers drew our names. We were motivated not only to attend Sunday school, but also to be judged by Martha as the best behaved child up the holler. (I think Miss Mary blew it one year, however, when my present consisted only of a bag of used marbles. Afterwards, I prayed all year long for God to forgive me for whatever it was I had done wrong.) We all prayed that Martha would put in a good word for us. Although attendance might be a little spotty at other times of the year, one could be sure that the house over-flowed on the Sundays nearing the Christmas season. To quote my Aunt Margaret, we all stared as if we had peas in our eyes when Martha's husband Dewey pulled up in his sled filled with Maysville gifts.

One year in particular I was specially rewarded. When I opened my gift, inside the package was a View Master. My excitement was little flattened, however, when I showed my gift to Granny. As she looked through the stereo-optic lenses and saw actors in costume, she kept muttering, "Just sinful!" Granny continued to look at all of the stories, however; and once or twice when I had been outside and came back inside from the cold, I found her going through all the pictures again. I figured Granny was looking for more evidence to convict the actors and sentence them to hell. Granny was an absolute expert in judging; and to her credit, she always stood by her rulings. Once she berated her niece Hazel Combs for hanging out discolored towels on the fence to dry. Granny's own towels were hospital white because she boiled them in clean well water before she scrubbed them with home-made lye-soap on her washboard. When word got back to Hazel that Granny had condemned her for this, she asked Granny about it. "Well, I sure said it," Granny told her. That ended the conversation, but it did not end Hazel's frequent visits to borrow salt or something else she might be out of on any particular day.

Martha had even more status on Long Shoal because her son Russell was also my fifth-grade teacher. Perhaps more to make his own life easier than due to meeting the needs of the exceptional talent facing him in the classroom, Mr. Gabbard decided to double promote three of us from the fifth grade to the sixth grade. He did not double promote Vina Stacy because when he sent her to the chalk board to solve some arithmetic problems, Mr. Gabbard's required examination for advancement, Vina could not carry across place value columns. Vina felt the examination was biased and staged a protest by refusing to come to school any more that year. (She also had not attended much before the test.) Either way, Mr. Gabbard was relieved of preparing any lessons for fifth-graders that year.

Mr. Gabbard's teaching did not exactly inspire, but it did provoke. One day in history class, he kept referring to the "Decoration of Independence."

"That cannot be right!" I exclaimed in my best legal terms, "That word clearly has an 'l' in it."

"If you are right, then how would you pronounce it?" Mr. Gabbard asked.

Well, I had not counted on this. But to support my argument, I proceeded to incorrectly attack the word phonetically. I slowly pronounced the word "Dee . . . clare . . . a . . . shun."

Believe it or not, Mr. Gabbard accepted my version; and all day long all of us referred to the famous document as such.

When I shared this incident with Granny in the evening, she immediately set me straight. She also questioned Mr. Gabbard's credentials for being in the classroom and almost for even being in the world. Granny, more often than not, was generally right about things; but she was a little quick in her judgments in my opinion. On this one, even though she might be right, there was no way I was going to let Mr. Gabbard know of her opinion. That Christmas gift meant too much for me to cross him or his mother. So our sixth grade class, including the advanced pupils, continued through the whole history unit with no correction of the pronunciation for the "Dee . . . clare . . . a . . . shun" of Independence.

The real reason for me easily to agree to Martha's suggestion to look into Buckhorn and Berea was my going to Lee County High School would hardly have been possible. A few others had done it, but none in the last seven years. For me to do so would have meant leaving home each morning at about 4:00 A.M., walking several miles to catch the bus, and then not getting back home until 7:00 P.M. in the evening—far too late for getting in wood for the fire and water from the spring. A boarding school made a lot more sense. I was twelve years old at the time and in the eighth grade thanks to my double promotion. For those of us finishing the eighth grade that meant four of the five of us in class were saying goodbye to formal education of any kind. This level after all was considered to be enough book learning for most people in our area. By this age it was considered more important to get on with work to support the family than involve oneself with useless, formal education.

My parents, however, supported my going on to school. I think my father was actually secretly proud of me. From his perspective, he likely also felt I would not be much good for anything else. To him, it might also have been an easier resolution to a bigger problem between us. My father was a good man, an honest man except when horse-trading, and a very hard-working man. He had two major character flaws, one not of his making but from his own fate of having been a physically abused child; and the other from something only he could have done anything about: alcohol. When he got drunk, which was periodic, the alcohol often did not mix with his childhood abuse. I have seen him kill cats, dogs, and even a mule while in his delirious state. While doing so, he cursed his phantom father. He shot my mother in the face as a follow-up to

9

the celebration of World War II, which brought a new meaning to me to the expression of "All wars are local." And once on an occasion when I asked him for twenty cents to get vinegar for my mother to make pickles, he responded angrily by beating me with a mop—just for asking. He then followed that up by taking a shot at me with the old sixteen gage shotgun. I escaped by slithering along the creek bed on my stomach. I left home for a long time after that to live with Granny, where I knew he would never show up drunk. Granny had that kind of respect, even from Irish drunkards.

My days with Granny Bowman have been the most meaningful part of my life. Life there was simple but afforded many opportunities for imagination. For instance, Granny did a lot of quilting. Her frames were suspended from the ceiling, where in the day time they were raised to allow people to walk under them. When she was quilting, however, they were lowered to chair level. I spent many evenings under her quilting frames. Looking up at the white muslin lining of her quilt, the shadows from the open hearth fire inspired dreams of all concoctions. Sometimes the shadows replicated hell fire. Sometimes they painted lazy clouds that allowed every care to just drift away. I often played under her quilt frames until she put down her bifocals and called it quits for the night. At that point, we stoked the fire by covering the flames with ashes so there would be some hot coals left to start the morning fire. Then we went to bed.

The fire place itself was another enjoyable project. Before the winter season began, Granny and I went to the creek where she knew of spots with good clay mud. We gathered the mud and chinked the rocks in the fire place to insure the house did not catch fire.

We also cleaned off the cemetery at the top of a hill behind her house. That is where my grandfather was buried. Granny knew the history of almost every tomb stone in the cemetery, which must have included the graves of perhaps a hundred people. Two head stones particularly intrigued me because the markers had the same names. I asked Granny about them.

"They were brothers," she told me.

"Why would parents give brothers the same name?" I wanted to know.

"They did not have the same names," she explained. "This one is Otis (pronounced Ah-tis), and this one is Otis (pronounced Oh-tis). " It was probably a good thing those boys did not live long enough for the social security office to screw up their retirement checks.

Once I came back from a solitary visit where I sat by my grandfather's grave and meditated. On my return, Granny asked me if I had been crying. I told her that since I had been named for my grandfather it would have been good if I had a chance to see him alive. The only time I ever saw Granny shed a tear was when she answered, "Alex, I miss him too."

My grandfather, I have learned, had a lot of Cherokee Indian in his bloodline. He, his mother, and two brothers walked and took turns riding their only mule all the way back to Lee County from Arkansas after the father had been killed by a lightning strike. Two older daughters were left behind.

A favorite story my mother told about her father involved his effort to get her to vote for a Democrat. She was resistant to do so. Her father then explained, "Edna, you have to do this. He is one of my very best friends."

"If he is such a good friend, Pap, how can he be a Democrat?" Mother asked. She always finished this story by adding that she had cast two votes for Democrats in her whole life and that she regretted both of them.

Granny's own past was something she did not talk about very much. My sister Mary's research shows that Granny's mother, Margaret Hiatt, came to Lee County Kentucky when she was only fourteen from Lee County Virginia, the county that borders Cumberland Gap in Kentucky and Tennessee. The trip is about 125 miles. Margaret rode in on horseback behind her mother, Mary Creech Hiatt, who at least thought she was a widow and who was making the trip to marry Jesse Coomer. Riley, a younger brother of Jesse, who was already married himself, fell in love with Margaret. From that romance, Granny was born out of wedlock. To rectify the situation, Riley's previous marriage was annulled, and technically Margaret then married her brother-in-law.

As noted, Mary Creech Hiatt at least thought she was a widow; but she may not have been. Her husband Eli Hiatt, a cabinet maker, joined the Confederacy as part of the home guard. He enlisted in what became known as the 64th Virginia Military Infantry where he ended up with the rank of 2nd Corporal of Company I. Home guard units were made up of soldiers whose primary interest was to protect their own property from either the Union or Confederate sides of the war. Most people do not know it, but in many skirmishes nine of every ten deaths in the Civil War came not from fighting but from soldiers trying to survive by living off the land, from lack of supplies, and from exposure. To survive, they often raided the stores of people whose territory they occupied. It was not uncommon for soldiers to even change sides during the fighting. Most of all, it was not uncommon for members of the home guard to leave the fighting for a while to take care of problems at home. This was not desertion; it was taking care of first things first.

As a part of his military activity, Eli and his fellow soldiers became embroiled in one of the battles for the Cumberland Gap. In September, 1863, most of the soldiers in the 64th were taken prisoner by Federal forces. Eli was wounded in the fighting and was one of those taken prisoner. He was then imprisoned at Camp Douglas in Chicago, a camp often referred to as the Andersonville of the North. Over six thousand soldiers perished there from starvation, scurvy, small pox, physical beatings, and exposure. Eli lasted only two months, likely from lack of any medical treatment for his wounds. His remains are in a mass grave holding those who perished in the camp.

While all of this was taking place, Eli's family never heard from him again. They all thought his life ended at Cumberland Gap. (My sister Mary and my cousin Steve Bowman over 140 years later learned factually what happened to Eli when they made a trip to Chicago and visited the Camp Douglas Memorial.)

Later that same year, in December, 1863, Union forces over ran Jonesville, the county seat of Lee County Virginia. Living conditions at home just went from bad to worse. Mary Creech Hiatt likely viewed the prospect of marriage and a move from the area to the Lower Twin near Athol, Kentucky as good fortune for her and her three girls Caroline, Orphie, and Margaret.

While studying for my classes at Long Shoal, I once asked Granny what she knew about the Civil War. I knew she was born in 1879, well after the War; but I also knew she must have known people who fought in the conflict. Strangely, she could report almost nothing on any particular battles. But she vividly recalled people talking about how hard it was just to get enough food to eat.

While she had little to report on the Civil War, there was one vivid recollection Granny sometimes talked about. It was the time she went to Jackson to witness a hanging. The execution was that of Bad Tom Smith in June, 1895, when Granny was sixteen. She said the whole family boarded their wagon with enough food for a dinner on the ground because they anticipated this would be an all-day affair. They left early in the morning as there was no set time established for the hanging. When they got to Jackson, an enormous crowd of maybe 5,000 people were gathered to witness the first public hanging in Breathitt County. (It was also the last legal one.)

Granny's version of the event, which matches the story printed in the *Louisville Courier-Journal,* sheds as much light on mountain religion as it does on public executions of the time. Bad Tom Smith acknowledged that he had murdered six people. On the day of his own demise, he wanted to get right with God. He told the authorities that he was having trouble clearing his soul over his final murder, that of a Dr. Rader, the leading physician in the area. Events that resulted in the murder began with Smith's courtship of Catherine McQuinn. She earlier had an affair with someone else in Jackson that so devastated her husband he ended up being locked up in the Eastern Kentucky Lunatic Asylum. The result of this bothered her new suitor so much he himself then committed suicide.

So Mrs. McQuinn was untangled again, which opened the door for an interlude between her and Bad Tom. A plot was hatched to get Dr. Rader to their house for an evening. Bad Tom's pretext was that he had become affected with something akin to the "fits" and wanted the doctor to observe him all night if need be to determine a proper treatment. The end result was that everyone got drunk, and Dr. Rader failed to wake up the next morning because he had a bullet in his heart. Bad Tom's confession was that Mrs. McQuinn emptied Dr. Rader's pockets and that he got nothing out of it personally—that is, except a death sentence and remorse for which he did not seem to be able to make right for eternity.

After much praying on the morning of the hanging, a decision was made for Bad Tom to be baptized. The entire throng of thousands of people walked with the party to the river. There Tom was immersed so hard and so deep that he almost strangled to death. Also, during the day a telegram was sent to the Governor in one final hope of avoiding the noose. In it, Bad Tom explained that he was an orphan boy with no friends. The Governor declined to intervene, which meant the execution was back in play.

All of this had taken much of the morning, so at 11:30 A.M., the sheriff announced from the scaffold there would be a break for lunch and that activities would resume at 1:00 P.M. Granny's food preparations certainly came in handy at this point. The break, the sheriff pointed out, was arranged to allow more time for Bad Tom to try to save his soul.

At the appointed hour, Bad Tom asked for as much time as the Sheriff could give him while he was on the scaffold. The sheriff said he could have all the time he needed, which turned out to be forty-five more minutes. During this time, Bad Tom made an extended confession. Granny's memory was not good on all that was said, but she did confirm that Tom blamed his present condition on "bad whiskey and bad women" and that he admonished the little children in the crowd to avoid both.

Bad Tom then asked all those in the crowd to put themselves in his position and to hold hands. Instead, each and every one there held their hands over their heads as he continued to pray aloud. At this point, Tom knelt down on the trap door and prayed hysterically for ten minutes. When he finally arose, he was allowed to walk around the scaffold for several more minutes.

Finally, after another short prayer, a song was sung; and the sheriff tied Smith's legs, placed the noose around his neck, pulled the black hood over his head, untied the rope that held the lever, and pulled the lever. Bad Tom dropped six feet, a fall that broke his neck. But just as the sheriff pulled the lever, Tom yelled out, "Save me, O God, save me!"

Just before the drop, Dr. Rader's wife held up her three young children so they could see the death of the person who had killed their father.

Granny almost shivered as she told this story. She said Tom flopped around for a long time like a chicken with its neck cut off. She was right about the time. Tom was not cut down until another seventeen minutes passed. Granny said she would never again in her life be a witness to anything so awful. To tell the truth, I am ashamed to say, the story made me a little curious. There were many times I brought up the topic again in the hopes Granny would provide more details.

This story was perhaps my first and still the most important influence on my involvement with mountain religion. At its heart, it was clear to me that feelings were the most important aspect of worship. If a person did not "feel it," no contact with the Greater Being could be established. Singing, emotional pleas in the way of public prayer, and fellowship with others in the service were all basic. If these things were present, there was no sin that could not be washed away at the river. Even if it meant a public execution, the crowd would be there to help the person cross over. These practices were in stark contrast to the Presbyterian customs I was used to seeing.

Another reason I liked staying with Granny was that it afforded me the chance to visit my Aunt Susie, who lived just up the road. I tried to avoid going there when Uncle Walker, who worked on a railroad repair gang, was home because just Uncle Walker's voice was scary. When home on leave from his work, he greeted me with a, "Come in, and make yourself at home. And I wish to God you were!"

Aunt Susie and Uncle Walker had seven children; but Ruth, Earl, and Dot according to Aunt Susie already "flew the nest." One remaining was Edna Willena, as the oldest child still at home. She had been named after my mother, who always hated the name because every one called her "Edney." I never gave much thought about it until in college I was introduced to the American poet, Edna St. Vincent Millay. My professor corrected me when I referred to her as Edney St. Vincent Millay, which he said just did not sound right.

Willena, fully into adolescence, walked to Tallega almost every day with a pretext of going there to get the mail delivered by the L & N Railroad. To get there and back, she risked her life each way when she walked the railroad bridge over the Middle Fork River. Because the trains never followed a set schedule, one never knew when the smoke stack of an engine pulling one hundred or more cars of coal would head up or down the tracks. If caught on the bridge, a person had just two choices: try to outrun the train, or jump down off the side. The latter choice was a far piece to the river itself if the person missed the framework of the bridge. This danger did not keep Willena from making the trip. I never understood what piece of mail could possibly be that important.

Granny never felt any daughter-in-law was quality enough for her sons. Since Uncle Walker was the oldest of her children, Aunt Susie had even more weight to carry. First, she was not local. In fact, she snared Uncle Walker by playing "Short Life of Trouble" on the five-string banjo when his work crew was fixing a rail road bed at Clayhole, in Breathitt County. Granny asked Aunt Susie about her parents. She told Granny they both had the surname of Clay.

"Oh, my Good Lord!" Granny exclaimed and asked "Were they related?"

"I think they were cousins," Aunt Susie replied.

"Well, I guess that explains why you do not have a lick of sense," Granny told Aunt Susie straight to her face.

The opposite was true. Aunt Susie had a lot of sense. She was the most independent and self-sufficient person I ever knew. Uncle Walker sometimes had to be away for weeks on a work gang during which time Aunt Susie held together her remaining brood of Willena, Garland, Carolla, and Albert. Instead of just gathering dead tree limbs for fires like Granny and I did, Aunt Susie took a cross cut saw with her; and she and Garland Jo cut down full grown white oaks. They sawed the tree into blocks, split the logs, and loaded up each child's arms with wood to carry home for burning.

My mother was very partial to Aunt Susie. She credited her with teaching her how to make biscuits. When mother worried the biscuits might be no good and stir the wrath of Uncle Walker, Aunt Susie consoled her by saying, "If that happens, I will tell him I made them." In the days when Granny's health declined but before she came to live with us, Mother and Aunt Susie partnered and stayed with Granny many nights despite the ugly comments that had been made to her.

Aunt Susie was famous for telling "haint stories" at night. She had a high pitched laugh that grew to a cackle when some poor innocent person was about to be attacked in one of her revelations. When she got into a story, all children who had piled into one bed—some at the head and others at the foot—pulled the covers over their heads. The girls were so scared that if they later needed to go to the bathroom, Aunt Susie had to get up and take them outside. The boys, who could not admit their fear, just had to hold it until the next morning.

A favorite game we played on rainy days we called Bread and Butter. Everyone stacked their hands on top of each other while a whole litany was repeated that ended with "the next person who smiles or bares his or her teeth, gets three hair pulls, three smacks, and three pinches." After the rules were announced, we had to look at each other until somebody burst out laughing. Willena was notorious for getting someone else to laugh or to fail herself.

When the weather was good, a favorite game we played was called "Annie Over." We formed teams on two sides of the house. One person threw a gum ball over the roof. If anyone on the other side caught the ball, then the entire party ran around the house; and the person who caught the ball tried to pick off someone on the opposite team. Tensions mounted while we waited for a return ball over the roof or an attack from one end of the house or the other. If struck by the ball, the person had to join the other team. The game continued until everybody ended up on one side. Garland, who could whiz a ball so hard and accurately he could have brought down Gary Powers in a spy plane, was a danger to be avoided. Carolla, nicknamed Midge, and I were no more than possum road kill; but we avoided being a target by asking, "Do you really want us on your team?" Albert, the youngest but a fast runner, was often the advance man for the team with the weapon.

Aunt Susie, whose hair had never been cut and came down below her knees until she braided it and tied it around her head, often cut my hair for me. Even though I had a cow lick which should have dictated which side of my head would have the part, Aunt Susie was adamant on cutting the hair to part on the other side.

"You cannot part your hair on the Democrat side!" was her explanation.

Sometime after my extended stay with Granny, I summoned up enough courage to visit my mother and sister at home. My father was not a person to apologize. The closest he ever came to it on the incident of his shooting at me was to say to me during this visit was that I should come back home where I belonged. I did, shortly before I left for school; but things between us were never the same. In that last conversation we had about what happened, I also told him that if he did not want to be my father, I felt no strong need to be his son. He let me get away with saying this because he was sober and because he knew what he had done was wrong. No doubt, my going away to school offered a way to settle this problem without either of us ever having to speak about it again.

My mother, on the other hand, always encouraged all of her four children to go as far in school as we could and was quick to support any plan that would further my doing so. One of her own disappointments in life was not being able to go to high school herself because her family could not afford to do without the work mule which she would need to ride to St. Helens each day. She loved school so much she spent a second year in the eighth grade, even though her previous year's test scores were some of the highest in the county.

So it was to be my choice as to the school I would apply to attend. At this time, both Buckhorn and Berea I thought were similar in their purposes and programs, which Martha Gabbard said was to offer opportunity for poor students from remote areas to get an education at the lowest possible cost. Students at both schools had the opportunity to work their way through.

The histories of the schools I later learned were quite different. My great-uncle Herbert Hogan, who bequeathed almost $500,000 to Eastern Kentucky University, much to the chagrin of some of his relatives who hoped his money would go to them, used to say that Berea became nationally famous for turning out "professional beggars." Uncle Herbert did not mean this kindly, but in a way it was a compliment to Berea. He acknowledged by his remark that many Berea graduates often have become successful fund raisers—for the school and for other good causes.

Berea, I have learned, started as a part of the anti-slavery movement in the 1850's on land donated by Cassius M. Clay, one of the founders of the Republican Party. Cassius Clay was a cousin to the even-more famous Henry Clay, best remembered for his efforts to solve the problem of slavery in America through the Great Compromise. (Through his back room bargaining, he was also the person primarily responsible for John Quincy Adams becoming President, even when Andrew Jackson had received the most popular votes in the election.)

Being a Republican in our family was a very positive qualifier. My father's parents were so proud of the party they named one of their sons Herbert Hoover, a name he carried right through the Great Depression—along with the nickname of "Hard Times." I once asked Uncle Hoover if it had been hard for him to grow up with his name. He verified he had many fights about it. But he also told me that later in life he had reason to be very proud of the name. While Franklin Roosevelt totally ignored Herbert Hoover and did not even acknowledge any letters received from him, Harry Truman recognized Hoover's excellent administrative skills and appointed him to oversee the food aid program in Europe at the end of World War II. My uncle, stationed in Germany at the end of the War, reported to me that Hoover's quick and complete work in getting the food distributed likely saved many people from starving to death. He said Germans had nothing but praise for Herbert Hoover and being his namesake improved his social standing immensely while he was stationed in the country.

Founded by the Reverend John G. Fee on Republican land, Berea College began in a one-room school and was designed to be a sister school to Oberlin College in Ohio, credited with being the first coeducational college in the nation. In fact, many teachers at Berea came there from Oberlin. The Berea program was based on the principles of "anti-slavery, anti-caste, anti-rum, and anti-sin." People with religious views in my area it seems had a much clearer idea of what one should not do than what one could do.

The school was given the name Berea after a town in the Bible as being open to accepting the gospel of the apostles, as mentioned in the Book of Acts in the New Testament:

Acts 17:10. **And the brethren immediately sent away Paul and Silas by night unto Berea, who coming thither went into the synagogue of the Jews.**

Acts 17:11. **These were nobler than those in Thessalonica, in that they received the word with all readiness of mind, and searched the scriptures daily, whether those things were so.**

Acts 17:12. **Therefore many of them believed; also of honorable women which were Greeks, and of men, not a few.**

During the Civil War, Berea's teachers were driven out of the county by pro-slavery sympathizers. But the school reopened in 1866 with 96 black students and 91 whites. Kentucky law later changed and prohibited education of black and white students together until 1950 when the law was overturned. When it did, Berea was the first college in the state to reopen its doors to black students. In the non-integrated years, the school made an even stronger commitment to serving Appalachia with its poor but deserving white students.

I witnessed the results of the segregation law myself in my years at Long Shoal. Even though our school was one room with fewer than thirty students, black children from the two Crawford families over the hill, who were next-door neighbors just down the road from Granny's, were not permitted to attend our school. Instead, they had their own school for what few months the county was able to hire someone to come in as a teacher. Granny, who was very accepting of the races except for marriage, used to take me to the Crawford Sunday School because it was close and we could walk to it. While there, I recognized several worn out text books we had used at Long

Shoal but had finally discarded. Granny always considered the Crawfords to be very good neighbors. But evidently the State of Kentucky at that time had different feelings with regard to our associating with each other to learn.

In contrast to Berea, I later learned that Buckhorn grew from the idea of a man with strong southern sympathies during the Civil War. While history shows that mountain people had little support for the Southern cause, I can say that I never saw a dark skinned person at Buckhorn in all the time I spent there—except perhaps for one boy who might be a melungeon.

None of this history was in my head when Preacher McClure and I set off on our journey out of the Long Shoal holler on our way to visit Buckhorn. I did already have a negative mind set toward Berea though from stories my father use tell us as we sat around the open grate fire on cold evenings. He told how Martha Gabbard, when he and she attended school together, could do nothing but talk about her own plans to go to Berea College. One day it seems Martha much to her permanent mortification passed gas in class. The fume, caught between her own over-sized bottom and that of the hard oak desk seat on which she was pinned, screamed for freedom with such duration that one could have plowed a row of corn and made the turn with the mule. Finally, just to cap off this major event in which the attention of every student in school from ages six to sixteen was fully focused, my father with his excellent timing duplicated her action by yelling in a high pitched voice, "BEE. . . REE . . . AH!" A great worry of mine was how would I handle going to Berea and keep a straight face, knowing of this incident.

With my ignorance of the history of the two schools, I was ready to try either Buckhorn or Berea if it meant I could get my education. School was my life and my escape. For sure, I was more than ready to get on the road when I looked out the front door and saw Preacher McClure's jeep rounding the curves and heading over the final creek crossing that led to our house. He only had time to say hello and goodbye to my family, and we headed out of the holler—off to see Buckhorn.

CHAPTER 2

Why Witherspoon?

The trip from Long Shoal to Buckhorn in 1952 took more than an hour, over roads of creek bed, hillside escarpment, asphalt, gravel, and finally, more asphalt. A good section of the road we traversed had been built on the same Indian trail my great-great-grandfather traveled in late September and early October, 1862 when he walked the entire width of the state of Kentucky.

During our journey, Preacher McClure did most of the talking. He did his best to give me advance notice of what we were going to see. He began by reciting some of the history of how my ancestors came to America by noting that the plantations in America we had read about in fifth-grade history were not in actuality the first ever plantations. Evidently Mr. McClure was not aware that my curriculum had not included fifth grade history.

"Really, the first plantation," Mr. McClure told me, "was set up by King James, the same person who had commissioned forty scholars to write the Bible we all read in Church and which came from translations of Greek, Arabic, and Hebrew." (This information came as a surprise to me because I thought what we read came directly from God.) "That plantation was called Ulster," Preacher McClure added, "and was located on the northwest side of Ireland. But most of the people who lived there were not Irish; they came from Scotland to live on the plantation."

I was then told that generations later many of these inhabitants found themselves no better off than when they lived in Scotland. So they risked life and limb to make a second move to America. Because they had little to start with, they arrived in the new country with practically nothing. Now I understood why people from our area are typically referred to as Scotch-Irish. They brought with them to their new country the clothes on their backs and their Presbyterian religion which they preferred to the faith of Roman Catholics, Ireland's primary religion. Knowing I had professed my desire to someday become a Presbyterian minister, Preacher McClure shared with me what would be required.

Historically, Preacher McClure pointed out, Presbyterian ministers were highly educated and well paid. When the Scotch-Irish movement came about (almost 200,000 of them came through the Cumberland Gap right after Daniel Boone's excursions), most Presbyterian ministers had no big reason to come along with the emigrants because they were doing just fine where they were.

Though the emigrants left their ministers behind, they did not leave their religion there with them. They soon learned they would need a seminary right here in America to train their ministers from the population who had joined them in their flight to the new country to seek a better life for themselves. Other faiths had already made this move, which had led to the formation of the famous Harvard and Yale Universities. The move to do this by the Presbyterians occurred in 1726 when the Reverend William Tennent founded a school at Neshaminy, Bucks County, in eastern Pennsylvania. That school was just a log cabin, and it was that school that inspired the architecture for Witherspoon College at Buckhorn. Both schools, Preacher McClure added, became affectionately known as the "Log College."

"History was made again," Mr. McClure continued to enlighten me," when in 1746, a group of Presbyterians founded Princeton, patterned after Harvard and Yale, whose purpose it was to train and send out a cadre of American ministers." Because of this strong commitment to higher education, the Presbyterian Church was somewhat at a disadvantage in competing with faiths that did not have such a high educational bar for their ministers to cross. "Hard shell" Baptists and the True Holliness [sic] Churches, for example, did not have this education requirement for their ministers—which explained to me why there were so many more Baptists and Holy Rollers than Presbyterians from where I came. In fact, lots of our neighbors found the Presbyterians to be a little too "hifalutin" for their tastes.

Continuing with his story, Mr. McClure noted with pride that Presbyterians and Princeton made a big impact on the founding of our country. Princeton's sixth president, John Witherspoon, was recruited directly from Scotland in 1768—likely for the 300 books he owned as much as for his great knowledge, which was considerable.

"John Witherspoon was the only minister to sign the Declaration of Independence," Preacher McClure added. I kept my silence on hearing this and instead reflected on how much consternation the pronunciation of this document had caused our class.

Reverend McClure relayed to me a few stories about John Witherspoon he himself had heard in his own training for the ministry. One he recited involved Dr. Witherspoon's love of gardening. On looking at his garden, a visitor noted there were no flowers.

"Doctor, I see no flowers in your garden," he commented.

"No, nor in my discourses either," Witherspoon responded.

We both chuckled even though I now doubt that I really understood the point of the story because I am not sure I even knew the meaning of the word *discourse*. I do believe Mr. McClure had patterned his own sermons after Witherspoon though, because his sermons though sometimes rambling and off-point were never flowery.

Mr. McClure's story only encouraged him to continue with his monologue. He had time to kill and a captive audience since there was no way for me to get out of a moving vehicle. He said that Witherspoon often had difficulty staying asleep at night. Because of this, he frequently dozed off at times he should have been awake and alert, especially after eating. To avoid being embarrassed by this during one legislative session where he was serving, he once made a motion that all daily sessions end before dinner. The motion lost. After the vote, Witherspoon rose and addressed his fellow legislators, "Gentlemen, there are two kinds of speaking that are very interesting—perfect sense and perfect Nonsense. Where there is speaking in either of these ways, I shall engage to be all attention. But when there is speaking, as there often is, halfway between sense and non-sense, you must bear with me if I fall asleep." This story I did understand; and I was beginning to worry about Preacher McClure's stories. I was beginning to feel them to be too close to that halfway point between sense and non-sense for my own liking.

I became more alert though when Mr. McClure got back on topic and informed me that not only was Buckhorn built out of native logs in honor of the school that became the first beginnings of higher education for Presbyterians in the United States, it also originally bore the name of Witherspoon College in honor of John Witherspoon himself who as a minister perhaps had the most religious influence on the founding of our country. Reverend McClure told me that all during its history Witherspoon operated only for a year or two as an actual college but this did not prevent the school from being known far and wide and even advertised as Witherspoon College for several decades.

I sometimes look back on this story thinking how much change occurs with generations that follow great people. John Witherspoon's great-great-great . . . offspring is none other than Reese Witherspoon, the actress whose biggest claim to fame perhaps is to have played country music singer June Carter in a movie—not quite the equivalent of signing the Declaration of Independence. However, in my own family, June Carter definitely had more influence and prominence than Reese's ancestor because we dutifully listened to June and the Carter Family every Saturday night on the Grand Old Opry—at least we did when the battery held out to power our radio.

In my own research on Buckhorn, I have found respect for Witherspoon College that went far beyond the immediate territory the school served. A letter to the editor of the *New York Times* dated July 16, 1912 perhaps best describes the respect the school had:

At Good Old Witherspoon

As The Times makes attractive feature of college news, may I present the announcement of Witherspoon College, at Buckhorn, Perry County, Ky., Harvey S. Murdoch, Principal, as it appears in the *Leslie County Banner* of Hyden, Ky., one of the few mountain newspapers of that remote region?

"Witherspoon has a faculty of eleven members. All grades are taught, from kindergarten to entrance to Harvard University. Next year it will open its own college department with standards equal to that of

Harvard, Yale, and Princeton. In the last year the girls' dormitory has been doubled, the refectory rebuilt, the hospital enlarged, a new chapel has been dedicated, and the boys' dormitory is being enlarged." That sounds thriving for a college fifty miles from a railroad, doesn't it? And what does it cost at Witherspoon? Listen: Room rent, board, and tuition, $7 a month. Count it—$7 a month for room, board, and tuition! Is that the Harvard, Yale, or Princeton cost of living? Yet Witherspoon has been in existence for nine years, is growing steadily, and there is no raise in the cost. Isn't that a record in this era of uplift in prices? Buckhorn, Ky. is a far cry in other respects from Boston, Mass.; New Haven, Conn.; and Princeton, N.J., but is getting there *prosus idem*.

W.J.L

New York, July 13, 1912

All this one-sided conversation from Mr. McClure lasted so long that we were now finishing the last eighteen miles between Booneville and the top of the hill that descends to the valley where Buckhorn is located.

As we did so, all conversation ended; and while I had time to think about my future, I could not help but also reflect on and be moved by the natural surroundings in which I found myself. May is without doubt the most beautiful time of the year in Kentucky. By the time May rolls around, every leaf on every tree has spread out to its fullest in emerald green, while the insects have not yet heard their call to wake, feed, and wound the tender growth. Summer flowers, especially iris and peonies, make every house—even the ones camouflaged with unpainted clapboards—look like a cover story for *Better Homes and Gardens*. Stealth rain clouds sneak over the hill tops, smother the valley, and suddenly explode with thunder and rain. Most of the time there is no damage from these showers, and the rain simply settles the dust and washes everything fresh and clean. Nature is just about perfect in Buckhorn in May.

It was just such a day when we crossed the county line from Owsley to Perry County and started our descent into the valley on asphalt. To me, this change in the road surface from gravel to asphalt was a positive sign from God that great blessings were about to be bestowed on me. Mentally, I compared it to the Israelites getting their first vision of the Canaan land. After rounding two or three sharp curves, my eyes popped when I saw lying in front of us a collection of huge log buildings—some apparently three or four stories tall—all spread out like the campus of a full university.

The first building we came to is one of just two still standing from the old campus and is spoken of as "The Log Cathedral." The Presbyterian Church of Buckhorn was one of the last buildings constructed on the campus—completed in 1928 and twenty-six years after the first building at the school was erected. The church became the centerpiece for the campus, first named Witherspoon College. Though I had never studied the architecture of a "cathedral," I immediately recognized the building as something special. The church is one of the largest buildings in the United States totally under a wooden roof.

Both the church and the other building that remains are the only reminders of the original campus. The church and the Geer Gymnasium were both designed and financed by Edward F. Geer of Brooklyn, New York. Though he was not one of the people who signed the original act to incorporate the "Buckhorn Association" in 1916, Mr. Geer and his wife were life-long friends and supporters of the school. Mr. Geer was a graduate of Adelphi Academy in 1889. Founding supporters of that school included such historical figures as Henry Ward Beecher and Horace Greeley. Charles Pratt was also a founding supporter and trustee. His name is carried on today through the Pratt Institute, one of the country's most renowned schools for art and design. Perhaps it was his education at Adelphi that was the source of Mr. Geer's interest in architecture which led to the design of his one-of-a-kind edifices.

If so, his interest in architecture must have been more of a hobby than a career. Geer became a very successful businessman, so much so that he was listed in *Who's Who in New York City and State of 1907.* He served as officer and director of several steamship shipping companies, including the Atlantic and Mexican Gulf, the Munson Line, Comerica Lighterage Co., and Henry A. Kessel Co. With the sinking of the Lusitania, it was ships like these that led America into direct action in World War I. Geer also became President of the Carey Printing Company, among his other business interests. As such, the company printed many posters that were intended to ferment support from Americans for war efforts.

Some prints from this company are now collectible art and can be found in museums in New York. The Log Cathedral is a primitive version of famous cathedrals throughout the world—with a huge apex held up by high beamed rafters in the center of the building. Below are rows of handcrafted oak pews where most parishioners sit during service. There are two symmetrical adjoining sides with more pews. If there is an overflow crowd, at one end of the building there is a second-level seating area that somewhat duplicates the choir loft in the front of the building. At that end also is a steeple tower that houses a bell from which a rope runs down to the lower level. It is said that from the day the church opened, someone has rung that bell every day at sundown. No matter where you are in the four or five square-mile valley, you stop when you hear the bell to silently meditate and pray—in "your own secret room." Both inside and out, all the construction is from native logs, which perfectly blend with the wooded surroundings. The church at capacity can hold more than 600 people.

The centerpiece of the building above the chancel stands

the magnificent pipes of the Hook and Hastings organ. Each piece of this organ had to be brought overland first to Mount Sterling and then by rail on to Altro. From there, piece by piece, the organ was carted the last miles by oxen wagon. In the early days before electricity, bellows for the organ were powered by young people who pedaled with their feet. There are stories around that during a dull sermon, speaking that is halfway between sense and nonsense, the boys sometimes dozed off and caused an awkward pause in the benediction until someone unceremoniously startled them into alertness. In later years, the organ was electrified, much to the relief of the person playing it.

On the day Preacher McClure and I opened the huge doors of the Church to peer inside; we did not hear the organ. Instead, someone was practicing with piano music for the upcoming Sunday service. From the choir loft, we heard the most beautiful rendition of "Whispering Hope" being sung by a young girl—I believe it to be Millie White—whose voice filled the entire building with notes as clear and crisp as the scenery we had just driven through. Preacher McClure and I did not speak a word but stood silently and listened until the girl finished. Then we quietly left the building to head to the next stop on our visit.

That stop was a visit with the President of the school, Dr. Elmer E. Gabbard. Dr. Gabbard himself had attended Buckhorn when he was younger and had become head of the school in 1936 when founder Harvey Murdoch passed away. He lived in the President's Home, which was also a log structure of several rooms that had great "curb appeal" by a porch that covered much of the front of the home. A story circulated among students attending the school in my day that Dr. Murdoch used to watch the goings on of many of the students in the school from this porch area. From there, he had a particularly good view of the older girls' dormitory Englis Hall. On one occasion the story goes he saw girls, too far away to recognize in particular who they were, throwing down a rope made of sheets tied together. Boys then were observed climbing the rope and entering the girls' room through the window. This simply was unacceptable to Dr. Murdoch. He continued to monitor the behavior until he learned the cues being given from the boys to have the rope thrown down. Now skilled himself in the entry system, he approached the building, gave the signal, and down came the sheet rope. Unfortunately for him, when he was about half way up to the upper level window, the girls noticed his bald head—which did not appeal to their romantic interests. So down quickly came the sheets along with Dr. Murdoch, as the girls literally almost broke his heart—among other vital organs.

My first visit to the President's home was far too serious for me to have enjoyed this story. Instead, Dr. Gabbard greeted Preacher McClure and me at his front door and ushered us into his office which was furnished with his huge desk and oversized stuffed chairs all surrounded by walls filled with shelves of books and records. Though Preacher McClure was acquainted with Dr. Gabbard and was at ease with him, his imposing figure consisting of a somewhat exaggerated but symmetrical facial structure, white hair, and booming voice certainly intimidated me. Elmer Gabbard was ruggedly handsome and imposing. I doubt he could have whispered if he tried. But he welcomed me as a potential new student to the school and briefly detailed the Buckhorn program.

Mainly he laid out the financial terms. "I was," as was every other student he said, "to work on the school farm full-time for six weeks each summer before school began in August." I was also to work fifteen hours a week on the farm during the school year. In addition, my family would be required to pay ten dollars a month for the nine months of the school year. I believe I became the last paying full-time resident student at Buckhorn, as most students who stayed on campus while I was there paid nothing because they were from broken homes, were on scholarship, came there in some kind of diversionary program, or came on campus from the surrounding area just for the days school was in session. The latter may have paid even more than I, but they did not have to work. Most of the former did work, though many did so very reluctantly.

After leaving the meeting with Dr. Gabbard, Preacher McClure felt I should also see the dormitory so that I could learn what daily living would be like in my new home. While all the other buildings on campus were built from logs, the "Big Boys" Dormitory, which housed those between the ages of fourteen and eighteen, was built from blocks of rock cut from native sandstone. This building had replaced the earlier dormitory Louise Hall (named for Dr. Murdoch's wife) which burned in the 40's, prescient of dreaded events to come. The materials used in the modern building made it into an echo chamber. On the first floor there was a foyer with the apartment for the head of the dormitory off to the side. To the back there were two dormitory rooms on each end and an assembly hall sandwiched between. The whole building rested on land that had been carved directly out of the side of a steep mountain at its back. This cut in the hill in the rear required a retaining wall taller than my head to prevent mud slide avalanches during periods of heavy rain.

There were stairs to the second level on each side. On this level there were bathrooms on each end of the building with multiple showers and toilets. Seeing this immediately caused me great concern because the showers and toilets were totally open. We did not have even an out-door facility at our home and our living quarters were close, but none of us ever saw anyone naked. Even though my brother Jimmy, older by three years, and I shared a bed a home, we never dressed or undressed in front of each other. Looking on someone naked from my upbringing was sinful. Around the stairs and bathrooms on the second floor, the dormitory had ten rooms for students. Each room had two army bunk beds holding four mattresses upper and lower and all were neatly made up with olive green woolen army blankets, two study tables, two closets, and a dresser with four drawers—one drawer for each student. It quickly occurred to me that life here was going to be as close-quartered as my own home.

Preacher McClure knocked on the dormitory head's door, but we found no one home. He decided we should complete our tour anyway. Not one student was seen throughout any of the rooms which were all tidy and clean with absolutely nothing out of place. We assumed everyone was out working on the farm.

In the center room of the second floor that looked out on much of the entire campus, however, we were startled to see standing in front of an open window a solitary blonde-haired muscular boy almost grown whose clothing consisted of nothing. Even though nude, he seemed completely at ease as if he had known us his whole life. Clarence said he was seventeen and had been at Buckhorn for a long time. Why was he not out working with the other boys, I wondered. Clarence came across as confident and as a person ready to meet the world head on. Indeed, I found out later, he already had. I believe he came to the school when he was just three years old. From his early days with some speech problems, he grew to become a faculty favorite, a good athlete, and a Chamber of Commerce kind of person for the school.

I learned many years afterwards that when Clarence left the school, he finished a military career as a Lt. Colonel in the

Air Force and also had success in real estate. I was also told that when his mother was buried in the cemetery that overlooks the campus of the school, Clarence did not attend. For many who lived the Witherspoon College life, Buckhorn—for all its good and bad—became mothers and fathers.

His confidence certainly was not the case with me. After my first look, my eyes stayed on the floor; and I let Preacher McClure do all the talking. I remember little of what was said by either of them. I just kept thinking to myself that I was failing at the one half-way positive thing I ever remember my father saying to me, which was, "Alex, I don't understand you. When we are out in public, you talk like you actually have some sense. But as soon as we get home, you act like you are dumb as Bill Bennett's goat." His comments should have bothered me; but they did not because when he said them I just reflected silently to myself, "Well, Dad, if conversation around here was ever about anything else but trading horses and mules or replaying a fox race by mimicking dogs barking, maybe I would participate more in a conversation." Right now, however, my reflection was that perhaps my father's assessment of my abilities was just about right.

The conversation with Clarence finally ended, and Preacher McClure and I headed home. On the way back there were more stories of John Witherspoon. Mr. McClure said that Witherspoon grew very impatient with the delay in passing the Declaration of Independence.

"But just five months after Witherspoon signed," Mr. McClure, told me, "the British burned his library."

Even that did not hold him back. He served six years in Congress and retired. His retirement was short because he was persuaded to return for another two years in 1780. He then took on the work of Princeton and the pulpit. One has to admit, he certainly had courage. Shortly after the war, for instance, he visited England in an effort to advertise the university and hopefully raise money to support the school. The trip it turned out just barely covered his expenses.

"Witherspoon was especially noted for his work with young people," Mr. McClure said, "and they gave him their full attention and took his words to heart." I was not so dumb as not to get the drift of what I was hearing this time. Reverend McClure's stories of Witherspoon were a lot like the reverend's sermons. He wanted us to get the meaning of his addresses without having to tell us directly what he meant. Sometimes that worked, but many times after he preached, I heard comments such as, "What in the hell was he talking about?" But this time I knew. What he was really trying to say to me was, "Alex, you need to listen up and learn everything you can if you go to Buckhorn." I mentally went to my "secret room" and prayed that I would be able to do so.

Preacher McClure said Witherspoon was famous for his "anecdotes," some funny and some meant for instruction, which I guess is why the minister knew so much about him. He finally got to a little personal information about Witherspoon, who he noted had fathered ten children by his first wife, five of whom successfully survived to adulthood. One son was killed in the War; one became a physician, and one a lawyer. The two girls married well—one to the next president of Princeton after Witherspoon, and the other to a "celebrated" historian named Ramsay, but who was not so celebrated that I had ever heard of him then or since. Witherspoon married again when he was seventy, to a lady who was only twenty-three years old. Ann, the second wife, bore him two more daughters. "Hmmm," I thought, "just like most of the people from my holler." (There were twelve children in total on my mother's side and nine on my father's, though there were only four children in my immediate family.)

As we traveled back to Long Shoal, there was also some talk of what it would be like to go to Buckhorn. Preacher gave me such positive comments in his estimation of my own abilities and work ethic that I "bucked up" and felt maybe I could make it there. When I told my mother and father about the trip, I added that Buckhorn was where I wanted to go to school and there was no need for me to visit Berea. My feelings about the school were not exactly shared by other members of my family though. My brother picked me up to take me home once from Buckhorn and commented when we got there, "God dang it, I wouldn't stay all night at that place."

Coming up with the ten dollars each month would definitely be hard, but my parents let me know that if I really wanted to go on to school they would find the money somewhere. My mother vowed that she could ship cream from our cows and sell some eggs and chickens to help raise the money. Dad felt he could sell at least one cured ham from hogs he slaughtered every fall, set aside some money he made as "boot" from trading horses and mules, and also earmark some of the proceeds from selling the annual tobacco crop from our six-tenths of an acre government allotment. My parents did come up with the money. They never missed a payment during the four years I was a student.

CHAPTER 3

Friends in High Places

Had I known more about the history of Buckhorn, I would have had very little interest in going to school there. For though E. O. Guerrant was not the person directly responsible for the founding of Witherspoon College at Buckhorn, it was he who recruited to his cause one Harvey Murdoch, the person who did found the school—a learning institution that was intended to be a mission to the mountain people whom Guerrant called Highlanders because so many of us were Scotch-Irish. From my own experience, I have become much accustomed to being called a "hillbilly" or a "briar hopper," but I can never even once recall being called a Highlander.

As a part of his mission, Dr. Guerrant began an organization he called the Society of Soul Winners. The Soul Winners were nothing more than glorified missionaries or at the very least, supporters of missionary work. At its beginning, according to Guerrant, the sole purpose of the Society was to find recruits for salvation, hopefully Presbyterian, but with any other persuasion being acceptable—except for the Mormons. In fact, Dr. Guerrant was so open-minded he referred to Methodists as being just as good as Presbyterians but who could sing better. The Society of Soul Winners he started ended up with an additional goal of eliminating ignorance and illiteracy, which it was felt would improve life for the Highlanders. To accomplish this goal, major efforts were made by the Soul Winners to develop schools, to provide medical treatment, and especially to improve the morals of those served. As a part of these efforts, before he retired in 1912, Guerrant and the Society were responsible for organizing thirteen "settlement" schools in the mountains.

All of these motivations appear to be high and mighty. I later learned, however, that of all things, Ned Guerrant was a Confederate! From my upbringing, this made him totally unqualified to accomplish any of the stated goals of the Soul Winners. Like the old lady I once heard during her shouting in church right before she began speaking in tongues, "There will be no 'struments' [*stringed instruments as per the Primitive Baptists*] in heaven!" my belief was that no good for God's purposes could ever come from a Confederate.

Nevertheless, some history of Guerrant is required for understanding the development of Witherspoon. Guerrant graduated from Centre College and began teaching at Flat Creek, Kentucky. At age twenty-three he interrupted his teaching to join the Confederate Army—after he had promised his own father he would not do so. To his credit, he stuck it out to the end of the war. In fact, when the Civil War was over, Guerrant refused to surrender in Virginia. Instead, he returned to Kentucky and paroled himself into the general population. Though somewhat frail, Guerrant was extremely fluent and was also skilled at handwriting, a prized talent in those days. In his position as a secretary for a General as well as other officers, he authored many communications sent from one Confederate command to another. Ned Guerrant kept notes of almost everything he did. His diary of more than a half-million words provides a pretty explicit and very expansive history of all the war action he saw, as well as events and even rumors he heard from other battles.

Guerrant came into the mountains early on in the war. He left his thirty-three students, forfeited his salary of $50 per month, paid his bills, and collected what was owed to him—leaving him with a net balance of $50. He bought a pistol, saddled up his horse "Black Prince" and said good-bye to his friends and relatives. Then the collection of soldiers who formed his unit immediately mended their way farther south and east and headed through the mountains to join the fighting rank— because at this stage of the War, "the real war always seemed to be somewhere else." His group was disappointed to find few recruits to join their cause as they traveled. In fact, there was little interest from most people in the mountains for the war on either side at this stage of the conflagration. After all, slavery certainly was not an issue in hills. In addition, the mountain economy was so poor it had little to offer to either the North or the South. Other than for the few recruits to the army, about the only contribution to the War from the mountains was the salt peter (potassium chloride) mined for use in explosives. We still use it today in firecrackers. For a time, the substance was mistakenly thought that it could curb male libido. The stuff can be dangerous when taken internally; and who knows how many mountain women caused the early death of their cheating husbands by giving salt peter to them and causing cancer or a heart attack.

In his earliest travels during the War, Guerrant saw first-hand the condition of the people in the mountains –enough to be moved to want to do something to change things after he left the military. According to his diary, in January, 1862, his group faced three inches of snow on the ground; so they stopped at the home of a Mr. Williams on Quicksand in Breathitt County. Just to get to the house, they had to cross the South Fork of the

Kentucky River by canoe while they made their horses swim the river.

Although they were welcomed by the Williams family, the living conditions the troops observed absolutely shocked the soldiers. The family tallied a dozen members. Their belongings consisted of a churn which was being used as a bucket for water. The churn was not needed for its intended purpose because there was no cow. There was only one fireplace to warm the dozen visitors and the large family. The girls crowded around half-frozen. The boys hardly had enough clothing to cover themselves. Though it was the middle of winter, the young children had no shoes and nothing to put on their heads. Their one cooking utensil was a half a skillet. The family had four chairs, three of them bottomless and with broken legs. There was not even a spring for water. Instead they drew their water from a muddy creek. Recalling scenes like this after the War and wanting to do something about it, Guerrant attended medical school and theological seminary and then spent much of his life in the mountains to answer what became his real calling in life. Time after time, he visited communities in which he conducted medical clinics in the morning and searched for souls in the afternoon.

Though almost a hundred years removed from the time of Guerrant's vision, things were not all that different in my own home that I left to attend school at Buckhorn. Our house had a lean-to kitchen and two front rooms propped up on large sand-stone rocks. It happened to be the same house in which I was born, but at that time it was located on Coal Branch up the road from my Granny's. Now relocated two miles away and seeing a second life, each of the front rooms had two double beds, one of which was always made up as a spare in case someone came to visit. Our heat came from a coal grate, and the coal came from a no-longer-in-use mine on our farm from which my father picked out blocks and brought them home by mule and sled. We spent many evenings round the burning embers, where it was plenty warm enough on the front side of one's body but where ice formed in pans not ten feet from the fire. The females with nothing to cover their legs were always "pieded"—spotted from the extreme heat from the open fire. We had no well for water. We carried it from a mountain spring which we shared with foxes, possums, coons, and an occasional bobcat. Fortunately, we did have a cow—two of them in fact. Mattie, a Jersey, and Tiny, the Guernsey—one or the other—was always "fresh." And there was nothing more satisfying for an evening snack than a glass of milk and a wedge of mother's corn bread made with meal from our own corn we had taken to be ground at the mill. Or for a special treat in winter—snow crème made from Mattie's high butter-fat milk. Even more improved than the plight of the Williams family, there were only six of us to share the space in front of the fire to enjoy the comforts of home. There were cane chairs for everybody except Thomas, a huge gray cat that persisted in leaping into my father's chair every time Dad left it empty. My father was strictly a fox-hound person and was not even the least bit partial to cats. Thomas knew this, but he was ready for competition from all comers. This on-going battle was one of the few times I ever felt my father was somewhat soft around the edges because I think he secretly respected Tom's courage. My sister tells me on occasion Thomas even accompanied Dad on fox hunting nights.

Guerrant's story of the Williams family and some of his other descriptions of mountain people would have been very offensive to me. In our family we had an abundance of pride even if we had limited possessions and comforts. In the case of his description of the poor Williams family, at least he appeared to be sympathetic. In other cases, his comments were just plain unflattering. For example, Guerrant once described a guide employed by his group as a "Crane-like person . . . intolerable except for his path-finding wit." Here his comments were getting personal. My nick-name in high school as it turned out was "Crane," because when I started my adolescent growth spurt most of it was centered on my neck and my feet. A difference though is that I never had much "wit" for finding my way along cow paths and got lost several times when my parents sent me to the store. Once, for instance, when I was nine, I ended up at Paw Paw instead of Robert McIntosh's store on Dunigan's Branch and did not get home until dark, and then only by returning on the main road instead of the over-the-hill paths. Instead of happiness on the return of their missing son, my parents were quite upset with me for having no sense of direction.

Guerrant once called Whitesburg, Kentucky, "the poorest excuse for a town I ever saw." He commented on a Judge Burns by noting that if the judge was as slow on the bench as he was in conversation, a criminal might have a life time of freedom while waiting to be sentenced. He had even worse opinions of the girls he met as he traveled further into the mountains of Virginia. He described a Miss Pack Boyd as "a large ungainly unintelligent looking girl with more bulk than beauty." He noted that after he left Kentucky (meaning the more "civilized" Kentucky he came from) and entered Virginia, he did not meet a single pretty intelligent educated girl.

But for all of his verbal condescension, Guerrant's greatest sin to me still was his being a Confederate. I did not know the Civil War history of my ancestor on my mother's side until I was grown, but on my father's side of the family there was a proud connection to the North that carries forward right to the present day—except for my brother-in-law Sandy Pitts from Mississippi, who persists in rooting for Alabama in football instead of The Ohio State University. He seems to feel the

North cannot claim a victory in the Civil War until some team from the Big Ten wins a football game against an SEC team, which at present seems to be somewhere off in the distant future.

In my family, our Union sympathies were directly connected to my great-great-grandfather, Captain David Hogan. He worked as a store clerk in Indiana and as such had good skills for writing and keeping records. He was only twenty-one, and worth $200 according to the census records of 1860, when he met and married Elizabeth Hawkins, a girl whose total family's worth was listed as $100. They had a one-year-old son named Harrison at the time Captain David volunteered to serve in Indiana's 49th—likely motivated by a signing bonus as much as for any political reasons.

Captain Hogan's unit was instrumental in one of the captures and surrenders of Cumberland Gap, a vital area that changed hands three times during the War. Because no supplies were sent to them, the unit had to vacate the Gap almost as soon as they captured it. By this time, the Indiana group had joined soldiers from the Ohio. Together they left the Cumberland Gap in a big hurry. In doing so, it was determined that taking any main roads north would be suicidal. General George Washington Morgan determined the best hope for saving his 8,000 troops was for them to travel on foot east of the main roads. Kentucky 30 today follows much of the route south from Beattyville.

Stories passed down orally in our family were that my ancestor was a scout for the Union army. In this role, he reported back to his troops that there was a mill near Proctor where the troops might be able to make hard biscuits for food. However, by the time the soldiers reached Proctor, Morgan's Raiders had already burnt it down. Guerrant even mentions one of these incidents in his diary entry of Friday, September 26, 1862, in which he noted that "Colonel Morgan and Captain Shawhan had been observing and harassing Federal Morgan near Hazel Green." This harassment and lack of supplies just about caused the marching soldiers to famish. They looked so terrible that advance notice sometimes was given to communities ahead of them so women would not see the men and be offended when the soldiers marched through town wearing little more than their underwear. Nature did not help either. The fall of 1862 was so dry there was hardly enough water to keep the units from dying of thirst.

The reason our family was in Eastern Kentucky in the first place was because of Captain Hogan, who in his scouting, escaped on a borrowed (stolen?) horse into the hills of Lee County from Morgan's raiders. During that flight, Captain Hogan was amazed at the magnificent virgin timber covering the terrain.

After the escape in Kentucky, my great-great-grandfather went on to fight in the capture of Vicksburg, and then to the Red River in Texas. Evidently, Captain Hogan's position in the fight continued as a scout. Two stories have come down through the years in our family to support this. On one occasion, he purportedly spent the night motionless and clinging to a high limb of a tree while Confederate soldiers camped below him.

Another story is that he spent time in the attic of a home near Vicksburg, hidden there by the wife of a Confederate soldier. There he remained when the Southern soldier came home and again departed, which gave just enough time for Captain Hogan to embrace the woman one more time and escape. Captain Hogan had a reputation for being quite a ladies' man. Evidence of this is provided by documented records showing he fathered twenty-three children.

When the War finally ended, Captain Hogan returned to serve in the garrison under Northern jurisdiction of Lexington,

Kentucky. Once his duties were finally over, he brought his family to Lee County to make his living by cutting that big timber, the same kind of logs used in building Buckhorn. In the four generations down to my own, a few of Captain Hogan's descendants prospered and improved their social and educational stations in life—likely not needing or desiring any missionary work from the likes of Ned Guerrant. My family was not one of them.

As is well known, war is often disruptive to family structure, even if soldiers return physically whole. That certainly was the case with Captain David Hogan. His oldest son, Harrison, who hardly saw his father as a young child, likely did not like so much what he did see after the Civil War. Soon after the family relocated to Kentucky, Captain Hogan began cheating on his wife. They divorced but reconciled. However, Captain Hogan's eye quickly wandered again. This time, a second divorce was final; and Captain Dave went on to start other families. Harrison, who witnessed all this, came down strong in support of his mother. His feelings against his father were so strong that when Captain David came to visit, Harrison for appearances sake directed his wife Rhoda, whose family emigrated from Virginia, to kill two chickens and prepare a big dinner. But as soon as he saw his father's new family coming down the road, Harrison left for the woods and did not return until the visitors said their good byes.

This behavior of doing the proper thing for appearances seemed to be a pattern with my great grandfather. My Aunt Cleo, perhaps the last person alive who remembers her maternal grandparents, recalls that it was common when she visited them to see Harrison sitting alone in silence on one end of their front porch and Rhoda doing the same at the other end. Whether this was evidence of problems in the marriage is unknown, for many people do communicate in silence. What is known is that someone once asked Rhoda why she married Harrison in the first place. Her reply was that she did not want to be a "fancy woman" like her sister Mandy, so the marriage appeared to be at least an acceptable alternative for her.

Mandy, the sister referenced by Rhoda, was an interesting character. She is listed on a census as being a camp worker, which meant she was employed around rail road work gangs building and repairing the road beds for the L & N. Her services were evidently more personal than the title suggests. In calling her a "fancy woman," Rhoda was using a euphemism for prostitute. Aunt Cleo says as a child she was so impressed with Aunt Mandy's bright dress, curly red hair, and her oversized ear ring that she wanted to be just like her, not understanding at all what that would entail. Whatever her profession had been, Mandy was very well thought of and settled down to a good marriage herself to Bill Campbell.

On reflection, it appears the durable marriage of Rhoda and Harrison may have been more of the proper thing to do than from an "I love you with all my heart." It should also be noted that Rhoda's four brothers had already left the area—to Arkansas, Missouri, and Virginia—as a result of murder charges they would have had to face had they stuck around; so at least her marriage provided her some stability in her life.

Harrison was a sensible man but somewhat autocratic with regard to his children. George, one of his sons, ended up losing a foot from an accidental gunshot wound when he was in his early teens. The story goes he was given a heavy dose of alcohol and then held down on the kitchen table while his foot was sawed off and the ankle cauterized. When the question arose as to what George would do to support himself in life, someone suggested that he could always become a merchant. Harrison responded with, "No son of mine will ever sell pencils at the courthouse."

With that position firmly stated, it was determined that George would need to become fully educated in order to earn a good living. This began with high school attendance at St. Helens. Arthur, his older brother was designated to look after him. The boys rode their mules together, and Arthur stayed with the mules during the day while George attended classes. Seeing Arthur remaining at the stable each day, a teacher told him there was no reason he should not come in for classes also. The gunshot accident led to both boys getting a high school diploma.

Because Arthur willingly took such good care of George and because details of the accident were never completely explained, some members of the family even wondered if the lost foot might have been caused by Arthur and not by George himself. As evidence of how much Arthur cared, there is a story of a baseball game in which a team came down on the train from Jackson to play a team from St. Helens. When the Jackson players saw George with his bad foot, they objected to playing against a cripple. Their objection began with an argument, but ended with a melee. When it was all settled, George played. In fact, when it came his turn to bat, George hit what certainly would have been an extra-base hit; but he was only able to limp as far as first base. Arthur followed in the line-up. His belt was a no doubter home run, following which he loudly admonished his brother, "Just walk it, Georgie, just walk it!"

A side note on the baseball game was that one of the best players on the St. Helens team was a black youth named Govan Crawford. After one of their games, Arthur and George brought home the whole team to eat. After everyone left, Harrison spoke to his boys, "This is the last time you bring a black person to eat with us. Nor are you to ever go to their house to eat."

Even though his own father had fought to prevent the South

from seceding from the Union, evidently years after the war ended, a Union person felt it was all right for the races to play together but not acceptable to so much as to sit down together at the same table.

Following their high school matriculation, the family decided that George should go on to college. Harrison decided everyone in the family would pitch in to pay for George to attend Valparaiso in Indiana. Arthur, of course, would go along as a personal attendant. George received a degree in law and became a permanent political fixture as the county attorney for Lee County. Arthur was just a year away from a medical degree himself when he was drafted into the military. After his service, he settled in Breathitt County. Though not a licensed physician, his services were much in demand.

A younger brother Herbert announced that he also wanted to go to college. There was no money for him to do so. He left home, against his father's wishes, and took training in telegraphy in a program offered by what became Western Kentucky State University. Later he worked as an operator all up and down the telegraph line. While stationed in Jackson, he had to take a gun with him every day to prevent revelers from shooting down the lines. He lost his employment when the Great Depression hit. Afterwards, he was befriended by his Aunt Mattie (who was conceived during one of Captain David Hogan's furloughs home from where he was stationed in Texas and named Matta Gorda, after the island which he was defending.) Through Aunt Mattie's connections, Herbert ended up on the campus of Eastern Kentucky University in Richmond and began taking classes. He sold tickets to ball games for money. While there, he again carried a gun when he served on security detail to the home of the university president, where students were creating a problem throwing pumpkins at the president's home. His telegraph skills were still in demand because Herbert was drafted into military service in his forties because of his knowledge of Morse code. Afterwards, he spent the entire rest of career life as head of finance for Morehead State University. He lost everything he had in the bank runs of the Great Depression; and afterwards he never borrowed even one penny, nor would he invest any money in anything other than U.S. treasuries. He credited the inflation of the Carter administration for making him a fortune. When he passed, he left the fortune—almost a half million dollars—to Eastern, not Morehead where he worked for decades.

My grandmother Hallie, a daughter of Rhoda and Harrison, was called "Flax" for her long, flowing blonde hair. She was quite popular at square dances. According to stories told to my family by Uncle Herbert, she should have "danced all night;" for when she was sent to help out the pregnant wife of her brother Willie, she came home in the same condition as her sister-in-law: pregnant. The child to be was my father Walker, but known by everybody as Rouster—and rightfully so. Although rumors still abound as to who the real father was, the likelihood is quite strong that my grandfather Wilson Browning (the namesake for my middle name) was not the father.

According to Uncle Herbert's story, Harrison, who could not tolerate such a shame on his family, arranged for "Wilse," as he was called, to marry Hallie. "Wilse" got a farm out of the deal—likely a strong motivator for him, as he was a very poor person. My paternal grandfather, from Clay County, left home himself at age sixteen and ended up in Lee County on his own. Everybody who ever knew him commented on how hard he worked and how skilled he was as a blacksmith, which in those days involved such work as shoeing horses, repairing wagons, and making plows. Although he always looked fine to me, in the eyes of the Hogan family, my grandfather was not over-endowed with looks. Perhaps it was because he was relatively short in stature, in direct contrast to the Hogan family, all of whom were quite tall—including Granny Browning. But he had a good reputation; and just as important in Harrison's eyes, he was available. The marriage was a proper way to prevent my father being born a bastard, which would have greatly hampered him from any social or economic success as he grew older.

To this day, there is dissension in the family as to the credibility of this story. However, to support his contention, Uncle Herbert points out that the marriage took place well into the fall after the weather had turned cold which would not comport to the date on the marriage license. Further, Granny Browning did not sign the license. My sister and I believe the story. Why else would Uncle Herbert make up such a story on his own sister, for whom he dearly cared? When my sister or I have problems with our relatives, we thankfully console ourselves by noting that whatever we are, we are not Brownings.

One thing is for sure. Grand Pap Browning did not feel all that positive about being the father of Rouster and had a bad taste in his mouth for him that even I as a child could sense. There was hardly any deal involving the two that Grand Pap did not try to stick it to Dad. Giving consideration to the likelihood that my grandfather's own upbringing had not been good either, it would have broken anyone's heart to listen to my father's verbal battles with his non-present father during one of my dad's drunks. Some of the abuse bordered on torture. For instance, there were times my father without moving as a young child had to stand in one spot for hours in the middle of a hot corn field and go without water or rest for no reason at all. The horse whip was more likely to be used on my father than any work animal. When my father was just eight, Grand Pap held him under water so long Dad was about to drown.

Hallie dug at Wilse with a hoe to make him free my dad. This event was witnessed by Aunt Pauline, just six at the time; but it affected her so much, she told of the event all her life. Grand Pap had a mean streak that carried over to many of his boys, but none endured the level of abuse that my father did.

Although he did uphold his end of the marriage bargain, after five children arriving about every two years, my grandfather became unfaithful to his vows. He contracted syphilis; and as was common in those days, neglected to inform my grandmother. While Ohio became the first state in the nation in 1920 to require physicians to notify infected partners, there was no such requirement in Kentucky. The treatment provided to Granny and Grand Pap was a compound that included arsenic and perhaps mercury to boot. As a result of the treatment, Granny lost all of her teeth as well as her hair. There were no more children for six years; but after the hiatus, four more came later. Granny died at age fifty-six from a twisted bowel syndrome, a young age for the Hogan side of the family.

I was fortunate to spend a summer month with Granny when I was only four years old. She was thin as a rail and very soft spoken. I had a reputation for being difficult to manage and was especially noted for having sharp teeth when I did not get my way, but Granny told my mother not to worry because she never had any problems with any child due to her much sought after recipe for "willow tea," meaning the use of a switch for punishment. She never served it to me even though I many times asked her how she made it. She always changed the conversation by saying something like, "Let's go gather the eggs." She carried them in her apron, and made me very proud by telling my mother how careful I was and that I never ever broke even one.

Mountain people perhaps were limited in so far as being

very civilized before the Civil War. With regard to my own family, it appears my ancestors were at least somewhat civilized. On mother's side, they were fairly prosperous in Virginia until the war broke out. On my father's side, there is evidence of good writing and mathematics skills. But history shows that following the War, there was great decline in the structure of my own family. The success of the three great-uncles in college showed there was a reservoir of cognitive ability. But for my own home, the level of educational attainment had declined to just finishing elementary school. As far as making a living, our survival depended on cleaning up new grounds, the use of bull-tongue plows, and tending to each individual plant or animal as a life-saving commodity.

Even though the North won the war, I can find nothing from the victory that personally benefited anyone I know. The cause was certainly worthy. The results, however, were devastating to not just my own family, but to a great many others in Eastern Kentucky. For instance, after the War, school attendance in Kentucky declined to half what it had been before the conflict. Nevertheless, I grew up totally committed to the side of the Union. And our family, from the time of Abraham Lincoln, has been true blue Republican. Our reasons for being so today have changed though. Our leanings these days are based on our belief in smaller government and reward for individual initiative. We see few people other than those with handicaps who are born with a right to an entitlement. We do believe strongly with charity from the heart. In my own case, the greatest compliment I ever received was from the parent of a handicapped child who in a news article commented that "Browning is the kind of person who if you ask to use his lawnmower, will come over and mow your grass."

To people like Guerrant and the missionaries he recruited, most people in our area were not very civilized. His experiences left him with the feeling that the primary obstacle to the lack of civilization of the natives of the mountains was due to their being "unchurched."

Some of my family, as I have described, would indeed have qualified on this count, though not all of them. At least some of my ancestors on my mother's side were named in Guerrant's *The Galax Gatherers* as instrumental for Presbyterianism in Lee County. In that book, which is a collection of writings intended to motivate outsiders to contribute to the mission work and titled after mountain women who gathered the leaves from the Galax or Lemon Leaf plants for use primarily for floral displays, Guerrant wrote, "A few of the hardy mountaineers forded the stream and crossed the hills to the little house of clever Matt Bowman, on the head of Twin Creek . . . . The generous mountaineer entertained nearly the whole congregation for two days, with bed and board, for the pouring rain prevented them from going home. . . . Here the first Presbyterian Church in Lee County was organized."

When I discovered this fact in Guerrant's book and read it to my mother, she quickly corrected the record by commenting that she was sure Uncle Matt had little to do with this.

"It had to be Aunt Callie," she protested, "because she was the only one in that house who could cook a lick."

My mother said she knew this for a fact because when Aunt Callie grew too sick to cook, Granny sent her to help out. Mom's oat meal and biscuits sustained Uncle Matt for days and surprised their own children who could not figure where all the good food was coming from. As we grew up, Mother tried to educate her own children to start whole oats with cold water if the oatmeal was to come out right. She never totally explained her good biscuits though.

Dr. Guerrant promptly set out to correct the problem of the "unchurched" population by establishing his Society of Soul

Winners. To finance his work, he wrote articles such as found in *The Galax Gatherers*, delivered sermons wide and far, and raised money wherever he could to support the Soul Winners' missions to the mountain people.

One of these occasions caused him to visit Yankee land where he spoke at the Lafayette Presbyterian Church in Brooklyn, New York. There Harvey Murdoch, a recent graduate of Princeton Theological Seminary and now a pastor of the Cumberland Street Branch of Lafayette Avenue Church came under the persuasion of Dr. Guerrant. To the disbelief of many in Brooklyn, Murdoch gave up his New York ministry and became the field secretary for the Society of Soul Winners. This position caused him to visit many of the missions that had been established by the Soul Winners. On one of these travels, he ended up at an outdoor service at Laurel Point, a small rise that overlooks the community of Buckhorn, where he listened to the congregation singing *Just as I Am*. He delivered a guest sermon on behalf of the Soul Winners. He also met and evidently fell immediately in love with Louse Sanders, who along with her nearly blind father Miles had organized the event.

A book and more have already been written about Harvey Murdoch. As a youth from Mississippi, he went to college in Colorado for the air in response to his health. There he stood out for his public speaking and baseball skills. Afterwards, he attended Princeton and then moved on to his ministry in Brooklyn, which he gave up to work with the far less unfortunate in the mountains.

Only one living person still has any personal recollection of Harvey Murdoch. Mrs. Jean (Keen) Wooton recalls his frequent visits to her parents' general store. "His everyday dress was formal," she says, and further adds, "He always wore a hat and a full length evening coat. When he paid a visit to our store, he never came up on the porch, but instead sat on the steps. There he would remain in silence for a long time, just looking out over the campus of the log college." Whether he was just meditating or admiring his accomplishments or imagining other buildings and services was not known. Perhaps the Keen Store steps were Mr. Murdoch's own "secret room" from which he prayed silently.

Mrs. Wooton also recalls sermons from Mr. Murdoch. One story in particular provides good insight to the way he worked. On a particular Sunday, Dorothy Kelley, a friend of Mrs. Wooton's sat near the front of the congregation where she accidentally dropped a pencil as she was rambling through her purse instead of giving her full attention as she should have been doing to Mr. Murdoch's elocution. Dorothy tried to retrieve the pencil with her foot in such a way as to not disturb others around her or draw the attention of Mr. Murdoch. However, each time she made an attempt to get the pencil, she found him gazing directly at her. First, she tried to pull the pencil back toward her with her foot. While in motion, she looked up and caught Mr. Murdoch's gaze, causing her to cease that action. Mr. Murdoch continued with his sermon as if nothing had happened. The desperate parishioner tried again, only to look up and find him once again staring at her. This cat and mouse activity continued for the full length of the sermon, showing that Mr. Murdoch was very capable of multi-tasking even during a quiet but firm admonition to all of his followers about the need to keep reverence to God in their hearts. Mrs. Wooton's friend sighed an air of relief when the service was over in the belief that she had escaped the full wrath of the preacher. However, as was his custom during the benedictory music, Mr. Murdoch exited the pulpit and came around to the front of the building to greet each person who had come to church that day. As Dorothy passed by, Mr. Murdoch firmly grasped her hand, smiled broadly, and wished her a good week with God by her side.

This kind of quiet but friendly persuasion made Murdoch a force to be reckoned with whether it was intended for someone not living up to expected behavior or to win a person over to support his cause. Clearly, Murdoch also was a person of vision and with unlimited stamina, which was remarkable considering his early health problems. He used all these personal characteristics to gain financial support from his friends from his Brooklyn days to fulfill his dream of a log college based on the forerunner of Princeton University. To start the enterprise, he first gave from himself. Murdoch donated part of his of $50 per month salary from his position as field secretary of the Soul Winners. He combined this money with gifts of $240 from the people of Buckhorn to use as capital for the job to be done to start the school. Of this, $200 was used to repair a saw mill. He then was able to recruit labor and skills from the local population to build the first of about twenty buildings that became the full campus.

Reportedly, Murdoch started his relationship with his wife to be, Louise, with a modest question of "Could you risk a friendship?" Evidently she could, because the two became an inseparable team devoted to the cause of Witherspoon College. On September 6, 1902, Murdoch, at John Gross's house, called a meeting of the heads of families in the Buckhorn Valley, where a declaration was drawn up and those present listed what they could give in cash or logs or building materials. The Declaration was a promise to contribute to the erection and equipment of a Christian College.

Although it was Harvey Murdoch's vision and determination that built Buckhorn, the school could never have been developed without at least some benefit of fate—that being Mr. Murdoch's connections with the Lafayette Avenue Presbyterian Church in

Brooklyn and in particular a handful of wealthy beneficiaries from there who provided both financial and moral support to the school at the beginning and for over fifty years thereafter. Harvey Murdoch made an annual trip to Brooklyn every November, and the local population in Buckhorn always waited in anticipation for news of some financial benefit that would be announced to them on his return.

Most of these Brooklyn people none of us knew anything about when we attended school at Buckhorn in the 50's, but several of them we did recognize by name because their names were attached to buildings very familiar to us, such as Englis and McKenzie Halls, the Geer Gymnasium, Albertson Hall, and the Lafayette Administration Building.

It turns out that the Lafayette Avenue Presbyterian Church has even more history behind it than Witherspoon College. At the time the Church was founded in 1857, Brooklyn was one of the largest cities in the country and not a borough of New York City. It did not become a borough until 1898. From its very beginnings, the Lafayette Avenue Church was filled with "foaming-at-the-mouth abolitionists." It became a meeting place for such historical figures as Frederick Douglass, Sojourner Truth, and Harriet Tubman, all born into slavery but who escaped and went on to become world-renowned activists. Frederick Douglass is remembered for his oratory and is still quoted today. One of his sayings could have been a motto for Witherspoon College: "People might not get all they work for in this world, but they must certainly work for all they get." Sojourner Truth—a self-given name—is best remembered for her extemporaneous speech on racial inequalities, "Ain't I a Woman?" delivered in 1851 at the Ohio Women's Rights Convention. And Harriet Tubman was a "conductor" on the Underground Railroad where, even with a bounty on her head, she returned to the South at least nineteen times to lead her family and hundreds of other slaves to freedom.

In May, 1864, the U.S. flag was raised over the church to remain there until Lee's surrender. It was taken down once— for Lincoln's funeral in 1865.

When I learned all of this history and the Church's influence on the development of Witherspoon, I put aside all of Guerrant's past. Like probably everybody else who attended Buckhorn, I am a devoted loyalist to the Purple and White.

Because of the influence of the Brooklyn parishioners on Witherspoon College, it is worth knowing a little more about the Lafayette Avenue Presbyterian Church. Right to the present day, the Church has a long history of social activism just as noted in its beginning. Some of this activism likely would not be supported by many graduates of Buckhorn and in fact is fomenting conflict within members of present day Presbyterians. In terms of the work of the Church itself, Witherspoon College is likely no more than a footnote. In total, however, the Church has been declared as one of the 300 most influential protestant churches in America.

In 1872, its founder and pastor Theodore Ledyard Cuyler invited Sarah Smiley, a Quaker, to be the first woman ever to preach from a Presbyterian pulpit. While the congregation took this in stride, the local Presbyterian authorities did not. Cuyler was brought up on "heresy" charges and accused of holding a "promiscuous assembly." The debate raged for days and was covered intensively by *Harper's Weekly*. Eventually the church authorities only issued a censure and backed down on the heresy charges.

Just a little over a decade later in 1884, the Church became directly responsible for the opening of Presbyterian work in Korea. Horace Grant Underwood, a younger brother of John Thomas Underwood who was the primary supporter of

Buckhorn, was the first missionary to that country. In 1950, Horace Underwood's grandson landed in Korea as part of the American armed forces in another conflict between a North and South that has not ended as well as our own Civil War. The struggle for Korea before and during the open war saw his mother assassinated and his father die.

From this early pioneer work in missions that came from the Lafayette Avenue Church has developed present day guiding principles of missionary work on the part of the entire Presbyterian Church. These principles include (1) preparing and encouraging those for whom the mission is intended to provide their own leadership, (2) building their own churches, and (3) governing their own fellowships—not under the missionary.

The Lafayette Church has gone through classic urban transformation with most of the wealthy and white moving out of the city and taking their membership with them. But the Church is still a strong force and continues as a hotbed of social activism. Today it is the heart of a predominantly African American neighborhood. The church has focused on such causes as sweatshop and child labor, workers' rights, and the ordination of gays and lesbians. It has a long tradition of providing space for civic, political, religious, and cultural organizations. Perhaps the best-known tenant in Church property in recent times is the pioneering dance group, the Twyla Tharp Dance Company.

The Church's interior is notable for its mahogany paneling and thirteen stained-glass windows designed by Louis Tiffany, although the original founders spurned any such ornamentation. In the 1970's the church commissioned Hank Prussing, a young artist from the Pratt Institute, to paint a giant mural around the upper balcony, reflecting the diversity of the community and the church. Prussing went out into the streets and took photographs of the neighborhood people and activity, which he used in painting the massive sea of community life he titled, "Mighty Cloud of Witnesses," a phrase from the letter to the Hebrews.

Despite this magnificent splendor, there is a physical connection of the Church to the more primitive Log Cathedral. The organ in use in the building today is an instrument built by the Austin Organ Company in 1910 (with rebuilding and enhancements in 1958 and 1968). But the original mahogany case and several ranks from an earlier organ were kept, a Hook and Hastings of 1886. The organ in the "Log Cathedral" as previously mentioned is by this same maker, though obviously a more simplified version. The bellows were operated by a powerful water motor, located in the cellar of the Church instead of foot pedaling by students at Buckhorn.

With the support of the wealthy donors of Lafayette, Witherspoon College flourished, adding almost a building every year for two decades from its founding in 1902. Some of those donors deserve to be credited individually for their generosity in supporting the mission of the school.

Perhaps the primary and most generous of these individuals was John Thomas Underwood, who was also the financial force behind his younger brother's missionary work in Korea. John Underwood became both famous and very wealthy by manufacturing typewriters. Initially, his business consisted of manufacturing supplies to support typewriters produced by Remington. That company, however, decided to make its own supplies, a serious mistake; for on losing this business, Underwood decided to retaliate by making his own typewriters. In 1895, he purchased the patent from Franz Wagner of Germany for a typewriter in which for the first time the print was fully visible to the person who was doing the typing. His Number 5 Model introduced in 1901 sold in the millions over thirty years of production. It would have been the equivalent of Apple's iPad of today. A state-of-the-art Underwood typewriter was featured in the 1939 New York World's Fair to represent the "World of Tomorrow." Buckhorn ended up being a part of the "World of Tomorrow Today" because the typing class at the high school featured a completely stocked room with these typewriters, still in use in the 50's.

Eventually the Underwood Typewriter Company was absorbed by Olivetti in 1959, which itself now operates in only a few European countries. Before its end, the company contributed to the World War II effort by turning out M1 rifles.

Present day remembrance of the Underwood typewriter is mostly confined to literary and film history. Famous writers such as F. Scott Fitzgerald, William Faulkner, and Jack Kerouac penned their writings on an Underwood. Films showing an Underwood include *Barton Fink, Moulin Rouge,* and *Whatever Happened to Baby Jane?* The most recent use was in the 2011 movie *Sherlock Holmes: A Game of Shadows.*

My sister Mary has her own humorous memory using an Underwood. When she took typing in high school, a frequent requirement included timed drills for speed and accuracy. For gainful employment, skilled typists in secretarial positions were expected to type sixty words per minute for five minutes with no errors. To accomplish this speed, students were taught to "sling the carriage" when they reached the end of the line. One day Mary was sailing along through a test for about three minutes—approaching a new record for her. When she reached the end of the line, she placed her index finger on the carriage to sling it back for the next line of type. The carriage did return. However, it continued right out of the typewriter and across the room, just narrowly picking off two students sitting in aisles near her. Though error free, her speed was determined simply on the words she had completed. Obviously, even with its high manufacturing quality, even an Underwood would not last forever. Suffering from a post-traumatic stress disorder from this incident, my sister gained more notoriety in high school for winning the Miss Junior Cook contest in Warren County, Ohio; and even today she has only a limited reputation for award winning typing skills.

Underwood had an impact on the skyline of New York. In 1911 he built a seventeen-floor skyscraper where two years later just a block away went up the giant Woolworth Building. He also built a second office at Vesey and Greenwich Streets, later the location of 7 World Trade Center. During its peak production years, a typewriter came off the manufacturing line at a rate of one per minute.

Above all of his financial endeavors, Underwood was a devoted Presbyterian and philanthropist. He and his wife, Grace Brainard Underwood, emphatically took an interest in Murdoch's work at Buckhorn. As a very important part of this interest, Underwood led action to form and incorporate the "Buckhorn Association." In 1916, the year this was completed, forming a corporation in New York required an act of the state legislature. Not only is the wording of the corporation important, the names listed on the document were very significant for the development of Buckhorn. The act reads as follows:

Chap. 188

AN ACT to incorporate the "Buckhorn Association."

Became a law April 12, 1916, with the approval of the Governor. Passed, three-fifths being present.

The People of the State of New York, represented in Senate and Assembly, do enact as follows:

Section 1. John T. Underwood, Grace Brainard

Underwood, Bertha Englis Sayre, James A. Smith, George M. Boardman, Caroline D. Barr, Andrew C. McKenzie, Frank Healy, Clinton L. Rosssiter, Charles C. Albertson, Joseph E. McAfee, all residing in the city and state of New York, Charles L. Reynolds, residing in the state of New Jersey, and Harvey S. Murdoch, Louise Murdoch and W. Francis Irwin, residing in the state of Kentucky, and their successors in office chosen thereto from time to time as may be provided by the by-laws of said corporation to be adopted, shall be and are hereby constituted a body politic and carry on the philanthropic, benevolent and humanitarian work and enterprises hitherto carried on under the auspices of the Board of Missions of the Presbyterian Church, at Buckhorn in the State of Kentucky, and within the counties of Perry, Owsley, Leslie and Breathitt and adjacent territory in said state of Kentucky and as may tend to the development, improvement, benefit and culture of the physical, mental, moral, social, and spiritual character and condition of the people of the mountain and rural districts of the state of Kentucky; to the relief of their needs; to the development, cultivation and betterment of their individual abilities and capacities along industrial, educational, and social lines, and for such purposes to provide, maintain and carry on in the territory aforesaid, churches, Sunday schools, educational schools, farms, mills, factories, a hospital and children's home and such other adjuncts as may be appropriate for the accomplishment of the purposes of said corporation.

Section 2. Said corporation shall possess the general powers and be subject to the provisions of membership corporation law of the state of New York so far as the same are applicable thereto, but without limiting the powers hereby conferred.

Section 3. The management and disposition of the affairs and property of said corporation shall be vested in the persons named in the first section of this act and their successors in office, who shall remain in office as directors of said corporation and be succeeded by others chosen at such time and times and in such manner as the by-laws of said corporation may prescribe.

Section 4. The said corporation shall be in law capable of taking, receiving, and holding, by purchase, gift, bequest or devise any real and personal estate, for its corporate purposes the annual rental or income of which shall not exceed the sum of two hundred thousand dollars, subject, nevertheless, to all provisions of law relating to bequests and devises or property by last will and testament.

Section 5. The said corporation shall have power to administer its work and affairs, from its principal office to be located in the city of New York.

Section 6. In the event of the dissolution of said corporation all its assets and property whatsoever remaining after payment of its debts shall become the property of the Board of Home Missions of the Presbyterian Church in the United States of America to be used by said board for its corporate purposes.

Section 7. This act shall take effect immediately.

First, this Act of Incorporation settled once and for all any holdover from the civil war conflict as far as Witherspoon College was concerned. Underlying it all, the final jurisdiction of the school was to be under the northern division of the Presbyterian Church, which is different from the support for many other mountain settlement schools. After the Civil War, for almost a hundred years, the Presbyterian Church had two totally separate governances. The faithful who supported the North became the Presbyterian Church in the United States of America, and the faithful who supported the South became the Presbyterian Church of the United States. Though the names were similar as was much of the religious dogma, the churches were governed in very dissimilar ways. The Presbyterian Church did not settle its own Civil War until 1983.

Several names on the Act of Incorporation appear to have been lost to history. But a few left their mark. First, of course, was John Underwood who continued to contribute funding for the school until his death in 1937. It was his backing that permitted the school to add much of the 1,400 acres of land and to develop its farming operations.

Another couple who made the school possible was Andrew C. and Isabel McKenzie. Andrew is listed as one of the architects of the 1905 New York Times Tower, which at the time rose to twenty-five stories and was the second-tallest building in the city. Though replaced in later construction, the structure of that building and the surrounding area epitomizes New York City to this day. We know it as Times Square. The next time the ball drops in New York on New Year's Eve, for some of us the Witherspoon College connection should be remembered. Another of McKenzie's buildings was the New York Telephone Building, and was the lone survivor of many buildings in a vast area that was demolished to make way for the World Trade Center in the 1970's.

The McKenzies had no children of their own, but Isabel dealt with this by adopting (not literally) practically every child she learned of who came from a broken or maladjusted home. As a token of her interest, she provided countless dolls to those children, most of whom named their dolls "Belle" because the gift came from "Aunt Belle." Her interest in Buckhorn resulted in the two-story Refectory, which in most people's eyes was the second most imposing building on the Witherspoon campus, just after The Log Cathedral. As the center grew, she also supported the substantial kitchen wing to the building. Isabel McKenzie died in 1951 at the age of ninety-three. A publication of the New York Community Trust, a charity foundation to which she left her residual estate, has the following comments: "All who had known her remembered her great devotion to the very young, but few could remember far enough back to recognize one probable cause of that devotion: Mrs. McKenzie's only child had died in infancy. And even fewer were those who knew that at some time Bell McKenzie had been in the process of writing a book of children's stories. The unpublished manuscript was found in her home after her death."

Another signer of the Act was Charles Carroll Albertson, a pastor at the Lafayette Avenue Church. Little has been learned about him personally from my own study. The library building on the Buckhorn campus carried his name. I have been able to locate a rare and out-of-print collection of poetry he published in 1905 entitled *Light on the Hills*. Of course, few people read poetry today, which likely explains Albertson's obscurity.

Albertson appears to have anticipated the death of poetry, but he stoutly defended it anyway. In the Foreword to the book, though not poetic, he makes statements in a short paragraph that likely could encompass a syllabus for a class in philosophy, also something not much in high demand these days, especially since pipe smoking is no longer in fashion.

> **"Poetry is truer than history. History records what has been seen and heard. The senses are less trustworthy than the feelings. Lyrical poetry expresses what has been felt. The Prophet foresees and foretells. The Poet fore-feels and forthtells. The Prophet and the Poet are twin souls."**

There was one person who signed the Act of Incorporation whose name I never saw on any building but who provides an interesting historical footnote to Witherspoon College. Clinton L. Rossiter, the ninth signatory on the Act, was the President of the Brooklyn Rapid Transit in 1916 when he signed. BRT was a forerunner of what eventually developed into New York City's transit and subway system. New York in fact in 1913 was struggling to develop a system of any kind. To get it moving, the City joined forces with the Brooklyn system and another line. The agreement was that all parties were to finance and build new lines, contribute money toward construction of city lines, and extend their own lines. The parties also agreed to equip and operate all lines as a unified system and to charge a fare of five cents for forty-nine years. That small fare did indeed last for many years.

New York City had trouble keeping its side of the bargain. Cost over runs and construction delays followed. Finally, a union strike in 1918 on the Brooklyn end of the business led to a wreck that killed 102 people. The BRT was forced into receivership and investors lost practically everything. Rossiter, of course, was not only an investor, but also significantly personally involved in all the controversy. These events are likely the reason there is little record of any further contributions from him to Witherspoon.

His grandson also named Clinton, however, became a professor at Cornell University and received a doctorate from Princeton University. This descendant is regarded as one of the greatest historians of the United States. His book *Constitutional Dictatorship: Crisis Government in Modern Democracies* forms the basis of thinking even today of what powers are needed by our branches of government during times of crisis, three of which in particular he referenced to include armed rebellion from within, economic devastation, and wars. (Considering the current on-going battle between Congress and the President related to our recession and the issuance of executive orders, his book might rise again on the best seller's list.)

Another of his writings, *The Federalist Papers*, is still used in high school and college history courses, though I cannot remember if it was required reading at Buckhorn. From quotes attributed to him, I believe the grandson may have been a Democrat. His opinion, for example, was that Democratic national conventions are generally more interesting and fun because the Republican conventions are too formal and business-like. He also explained the higher number of Democrat voters in the country by saying Republicans "sleep in twin beds." Sadly, this person suffered from depression and took his own life.

Until his death in 1935, Harvey Murdoch spent his life devoted to fulfilling the "objects" of the incorporated Act of the Buckhorn Association. His work did not end up with an institution that actually functioned as Witherspoon College, although Mr. Murdoch's follow-up leader Elmer E. Gabbard did make an attempt for a year or two to initiate college work when he took over. A booklet of information on the program was developed by Dr. Gabbard shortly after he became head. It was still in use as the primary public relations brochure more than a decade later. At the time of publication, the booklet noted that in its history more than 4,500 students within a radius of 50 miles had enrolled, of which approximately 600 had become teachers. Buckhorn had the largest rural Presbyterian Church in Kentucky with a membership of 561. Worthington and McDowell Homes, primarily designed as orphanages, were built to accommodate up to fifty children—and had a waiting list. Brainard Hospital (named for the wife of John Underwood) was staffed by a trained physician and nurse. Over the years, it services were used primarily for maternity needs and for the treatment of accidents and gunshot wounds. In coordination with the state and federal government, it also functioned as a treatment center for the scourge of hook worm, which often results in low birth weight, morbidity, anemia, and cognitive problems. (By the time my generation came along, we inherited the results of the scientific progress of this work. Our parents regularly administered to us a dose of castor oil any time our spirits were low and we appeared to be "wormy.") The farm served both as a means of support to the school and as a model for those in the area. And A.C. Harrington, Superintendent of Buildings and Construction for Berea College, described the gymnasium as "unusually commodious for a school its size." He admired the "rugged simplicity" of the facility. In all, a sum of $203,000 had been spent on land and buildings. For a time at least, the goals of the Society of Soul Winners were achieved.

Nothing was built at Buckhorn during my stay there, though there were emergency relocations from one building to another. All the previous building endowed those of us on campus during these years we attended with much of the atmosphere of Guerrant and Murdoch and perhaps with even a little of the learning and moral development the founders intended.

Documentation of Buckhorn's history is sparse for the years 1902-1956. Mostly, all that has survived in written form are the yearly reports given to the directors of the Buckhorn Association, and these are stored on microfilm at Berea College. There one can spend hours in the college library rummaging through the minutes of the Association meetings.

Those of us attending school at Buckhorn from 1952 to 1956 did not realize it as it happened, but we were the Last Souls of Witherspoon. Review of the records from the Buckhorn Association indicate the benefactors appeared to think of everything in planning for the institution, even to the provision of electricity when there was not any around. Buckhorn not only served people in the area, it became an economic force in its own right. The signers of the Act of Incorporation thought of everything except one: Fire.

The Family Connection:

Maternal Grandparents—
Cora Coomer

Alex Bowman

Edna (Browning) Hogan in 2008.
Edna made more than fifty quilts.
All were gifts except for the first
one, which she sold to buy a
Christmas present for her husband.

Mother:
Edna Browning in 1956

The Family Connection:

Paternal Grandparents. Wilson Browning and Hallie Browning holding daughter Juanita

Walker Browning and Jim Bowman

Walker Browning with Tennessee Walking Horse

Our family home at the head of Hope Road

The Family Connection:

My Siblings. James Browning. Joyce Ann (Browning) Pitts.

Mary Alice (Browning) Pare standing on
Hope Road and holding nephew David

The Stages of Man:

Pictures of my childhood.
Stage 1: Infancy. Conflict:
Basic trust vs. mistrust;
Resolution: Hope. Stage
2: Conflict: Autonomy vs.
shame; Resolution: Will to do
and development of physical
ability. Stage 3: Conflict:
Initiative vs. guilt; Resolution:
Purpose in life; humor.
Stage 4: Conflict: Industry
vs. inferiority; Resolution:
Competence and humility.

The Long Shoal Connection:

*The France House taken by adverse possession by Meg Greer
family as a result of my family's "mountain feud."*

*Long Shoal Elementary marching
at the Lee County Fair in 1950.*

*My brother Jimmy and
cousin Benny Paul Gabbard.*

The Stages of Man:

*My high school and college years. Stage 5: Conflict:
Identity and Confusion; Resolution: Fidelity and peer
relationships. Future Farmers of America.*

*High school sophomore class picture. College photo.
College picture with good friend Penny Jones.*

The Stages of Man:

Pictures of adulthood. Stage 6: Conflict: Intimacy vs. isolation; Resolution: Love and the sense of tenderness in relationships

The Stages of Man:

Breathitt: An educator who 'never learned to play politics'

Alex Browning said he resigned as superintendent in Breathitt County in June because board members wanted more control over hiring so they could award jobs based on politics and patronage.

When he resisted, the resulting controversy hindered progress, Browning said at the time.

Board members, however, said they simply wanted to find the people who were best qualified for the jobs.

Larry Hudson, former president of an elementary school PTA in the county, said Browning was right to resign because the split was hurting the schools.

"He just never did learn how to play Breathitt County politics," Hudson said.

When Browning announced his resignation, the local newspaper, The Jackson Times, said in an editorial:

"Superintendent Alex Browning resigned this week, the same week that the Breathitt County school system was lauded in the state's accreditation report.

"How ironic.

"Just when things appeared to be on the verge of getting better, politics, as usual, interfered, depriving us of what may have been one of the best things ever to happen to our school system."

Resignation and Retirement.
Stage 7—Resignation from
Breathitt County Schools in
1993: Conflict: generativity
vs. stagnation; Resolution:
Care and concern for others.
Stage 8—Retirement and work
on my 1840 home in Ohio:
(Conflict: integrity vs. despair;
Resolution: Reflection on and
acceptance of one's life.

The Edward F. Geer Connection:

S.S. American Legion

With a ceiling of unusual height and frequent windows, the dining room is an exceptionally pleasant, cool and refreshing apartment in which to dine

Edward Geer was a successful businessman from Brooklyn who was involved in steam ships and printing. He designed and paid for The Log Cathedral and the Geer Gymnasium, the only buildings of the original campus that still stand. On her death in 1954, Mrs. Geer left $10,000 to the Buckhorn Association.

The Edward F. Geer Connection

ALL THAT REMAINS. The Geer Gymnasium, built in 1924, and The Log Cathedral, built in 1928.

The Lafayette Avenue Connection

Brooklyn Presbyterian Church (1906); Organ
with Hank Prussing mural.
The Underwood Connection: *John T. Underwood was the*
largest benefactor to Witherspoon College. Underwood Towers.
Typewriter manufacturing Plant. No. 5 Typewriter

The McKenzie Connection:

Andrew McKenzie was an architect for the original Times Square Building. He and his wife Isabel funded McKenzie Hall, the Refectory. Burned Buildings: *In the spring of 1953, Englis Hall, McKenzie Hall, and Faith Hall burned. The Worthington Hall for Little Girls and Louise Hall Dormitory (not shown) for boys had previously burned. (Buckhorn Photos from the Buckhorn Children's Center Photographic Collection, Berea College Southern Appalachian Archives)*

The Keen Connection:

Jean (Keen) Wooton, the last person to actually know Harvey Murdoch

The Keen Home.
The Keen Store

The "modern" Boys Dormitory.

Learning for Life:

Lafayette Hall, the high school

Albertson Hall, the library, where I had my one-minute Latin Class.

Grundy Farm and "model" barn. The morning milk crew in 1936.
(Photos from the Buckhorn Children's Center Photographic
Collection, Berea College Southern Appalachian Archives.

CHAPTER 4

The Future of Farming and Keen Comfort

Until mid-summer of 1952, I continued to help out with the crops at home and gather wood for my mother to build fires for canning and cooking and washing clothes. I continued to stay with Granny Bowman as much as I could, as she lived alone and was in poor health. For almost a full year at the end of her life, Granny had major trouble at night during which time she constantly groaned and cried out but was unable to say what was really hurting her. It was a failing heart.

Aunt Grace, my mother's sister, sent my cousin Nancy to stay with Granny. Nancy, her younger sister Norma, and I were inseparable playmates during the year both our mothers separated from their cheating husbands. While our fathers remained in Ohio to work and carry on with other women, Aunt Grace and my mother moved the children back to Kentucky. In our play, the three of us invented two imaginary associates—Reatha and Lobba. Psychologists would have a field day analyzing the pretend things we did to those two people. On one occasion, for example, we electrocuted Lobba. I do not recall what her crime was.

A favorite memory the three of us have of that year is our attempts to cross a rising creek at a time when I was the only one with boots. We crossed with dry feet by one wading over to the other side and then throwing the boots back to the next in line. When it came her turn, both Norma and my boots almost washed away. Several times after that, Nancy and I questioned whether we should have offered prayers to have Norma safely cross the creek or for her to just cross over. With her unchecked innocence, Norma's behavior was sometimes nothing more than a display of outright insensitivity. For instance, Granny always saved her peanut butter jars that came in barrel shaped glasses. Because of their shape, we called the glasses "belly busters." When Norma came to visit Granny, she immediately looked for something to eat. To go with whatever else she found, she also asked for a glass of milk in one of those special glasses. Norma then followed up with a question of "Granny, when you die, can I have this glass?" (Norma later in life chose as her career the caring field of nursing.)

Following the year of separation, Aunt Grace and her children returned to Ohio for good. My father reformed his ways, and our family also moved back to Ohio. But after just another year, by a "democratic vote" of five to one, the decision was made for the entire family to return to Kentucky. Mine was the one minority ballot because I did not want to leave my school in South Lebanon. My report card for that year in Ohio shows A's in all subjects except for a B+ in Geography and History, and a C+ in music. I recall to this day the time I almost drifted off to sleep in music class and did not join in the choral activities. As the period ended, the teacher commented, "Class, this has been the best music class we have had all year." Evidently the mark of Average was really a gift from the teacher. My grades in Conduct and Application were also B's, sometimes on the lower end of a B.

When Nancy came to help, Granny would not let her do anything, including even wash the dishes. This job was a real concern to Granny because she had a wonderful set of fine white china that that been sent to her from Japan by another niece, Geraldine Igo, whose husband was stationed there in the military. Although Granny always wanted her to, Mother was almost afraid to drink coffee from the delicate cups for fear one would get broken. The only piece of that china that ever got broken was by Granny herself. Mother commented to her at the time, "Thank God, it was you and not me."

When anything was to be done for Granny while Nancy was there to help, it got done by me—at the specific request of Granny. I felt sorry for Nancy, who came with the best of intentions. But that was Granny's way. She only seemed to be able to give her love to one of her grandchildren at a time. During this period, it was my time. (When Granny died, my greedy Aunt Hattie immediately laid claims on the china, though she had absolutely no right to it. To this day, I cannot recall anybody else wanting it, only that no one wanted her to get it.)

Granny expected me to feed her horse Maude, who controlled much of the daily living routine at the house. Maude only walked—at her own pace—and trotted, which made her a two-gaited horse and which did not at all qualify her as being a horse worth keeping. Technically, Maude probably was three-gaited because she likely could also gallop, though I never saw her expend enough energy to prove whether she had that ability or not. To meet criteria for "worth keeping" in our house, a horse had to be able to move with five gaits—like my mother's favorite, Tillie, a yellow and black Tennessee Walking horse. Maude's fastest pace was a trot and a very rough one at that. She used this gait at her own discretion and generally when she wanted to make me uncomfortable on the occasions I rode bareback behind Granny who sat more comfortably in her padded side saddle.

Maude was locally infamous for her antics to avoid carrying Granny to the store. Granny devoted much of her time on store days planning how to tightly secure the saddle on Maude. Eventually, she solved the problem by first tying Maude to the porch railing and then putting the saddle on her. When she tightened the girt, Maude inhaled but did not exhale until her stomach swelled to at least three inches more than normal. Had she gotten away with this, when Granny saddled up, she would have hit the ground in short order; for Maude could then breathe out, shrink her stomach, and loosen the girt.

Granny got wise to Maude. After tying her up, Granny went back into the house and pretended to go on with her house work, often singing in her best off-key voice, "Will the Circle Be Unbroken?"—a song Granny selected for a lot more meaning than the original intention of the song, mourning the loss of a family member. It should also be noted that Granny's best singing was always very much off-key, a genetic trait passed on to me—and an explanation for my C+ in music. Further, no matter the melody, every song Granny sang sounded alike. Although she was not Presbyterian, on this trait she would have met Guerrant's criteria for being so. On the other hand, she would have been banned from the Methodist Church. Granny was non-denominational, so it would not have made any difference to her.

Maude, of course, could only hold so much air and just for so much time. When Granny surmised her horse had let out the air, she abruptly stopped singing and rushed out of the house, shouting, "I've got you now, you old strumpet!" "Strumpet" was about the worst word Granny used, but she did voice it frequently if she was upset at some person or thing. Anyway, Granny solved the saddling problem with Maude by grabbing the girt and securing it tightly before Maude could perform her swelling act again. While Maude lost this battle, she never surrendered the war and got some revenge by doing the roughest trot she could on the way to the store.

I had learned to milk a cow, which, of course, my visiting cousin could not do. So this chore also fell to me. Perhaps the single skill that I had that no one else in my family ever possessed was that I could milk with both hands. Granny was very complimentary about this. She herself had developed arthritis in her fingers, and many times she would have to stop her milking and straighten out the fingers of her milking hand with her other fingers before she could finish with her cow Daisy. Daisy and Maude must have formed a secret pact; they both had the same temperament. Daisy would let you milk just as long as she had food in front of her. When the food was gone, so was Daisy. She was highly surprised when with both hands I got my job done before she completed her treat. It became a race between us—whether she could eat her food first or whether I could finish with the milking. I am proud to say that I almost always won this competition. Little did I know that later at Buckhorn my one talent would lead to so much consternation.

Granny had another animal with charter rights to the Maude and Daisy team. It was her cat Tom. Though Granny insisted he not stay in the house, Tom made every effort to dart through the door every time it opened. This was nothing more than an evil game he played. I have seen him rush in the kitchen door and immediately out the front door if it was open. He almost tripped Granny as he rushed by her feet when she met him at the door with her broom. One evening as we went upstairs to sleep on the corn shuck bed that Granny used in the summer time to keep cool, the cat followed us. Granny grabbed Tom, opened the one window in the room, and blasted him outside, while at the same time insulting his gender by calling him an "old strumpet." This saddened me because it seemed Tom had not done so much wrong that he should be executed. I was much relieved the next morning, however, when Granny opened her kitchen door and Tom darted in just like nothing had ever happened. I can attest that the old adage about a cat always landing on its feet is true.

Granny did have one animal on her own team—all day long and every day of the year. Her devoted dog Wimpy, a mixed shepherd, was with her every minute during all those nights she cried out. Later, when my parents brought Granny to live with us, Wimpy stayed behind, searching for her, guarding the house, and patiently waiting for her to return. Finally our own dog Bruce went over to Granny's house on his own and shortly after came trotting up the road to our house with Wimpy following close behind. In my opinion, Maude, Daisy, and Tom each could have learned a thing or two from Wimpy.

I had just turned thirteen in June when my dad brought me to Buckhorn to start my summer work obligation. We stopped off to pay my tuition to Dr. Gabbard, and then I checked into the dormitory. There we were met by Scott Johnson and his wife Rhoda. Mr. Johnson was a somewhat elderly man who had a limp and walked with a cane. The cause of his condition remained a mystery to me for all the time I was at Buckhorn. But the thumping of his cane served as a warning to us if he wandered through the dormitory at night. Was he coming to call us down and punish us for something we had done? Or was he stopping off to meet with some of his favorites "just for evening conversation"? His wife Rhoda, with a stocky build and a matronly-look, I best remember for her habit of constantly clearing her throat. The Johnsons said little as they assigned me to my room, which was upstairs and second in from the East end of the building. Mr. Johnson did assure my father that I would be looked after and that he would keep me out of trouble. These were wasted words to Dad; for despite our problems, my father I am confident would have described me as a good child—even if he did not have a clue as to what went on in my head.

Dad had to get home, so he left me to spend the rest of the day unpacking my things. For the rest of the summer, I was assigned to room with Bobby Devault, a boy just a year older than I, who I learned had two younger brothers and an older sister at Buckhorn, and whose mother Violet was in charge of the "Little Boys" dormitory. Bobby and I would be the youngest of the boys housed in our dormitory because the cut-off age was supposed to be fourteen. Evidently I presented a little bit of a quandary for the school. I was a little young for the Big Boys Dormitory; but I was also in high school, which was another cut off point and which made me ineligible to live in the Little Boys Dormitory. Bobby greeted me with friendliness and made idle conversation as I unpacked. He then and for all the years I knew him never seemed too positive about much of anything, but his pessimism never seemed to be personally directed at me. Research in psychology has led to the scientific conclusion that depressed people actually have the clearest vision of the real world—especially as compared with eternal optimists who often perceive things through rose-colored glasses. This clear vision may be the reason why people get depressed in the first place. I would not classify Bobby as depressed, but he did have a much clearer vision of Buckhorn than I—certainly he knew the internal workings of the school. To protect his mother's position, he saw and just mostly endured. Also, because he had the benefits of time spent at Buckhorn, Bobby's perceptions then and now were and are likely better than my own.

My stay at Buckhorn was brief before I got myself in real trouble. Down the road from the main campus lived an elderly woman known to everyone as Sis McIntosh. Martha Gabbard knew her from somewhere and made sure I also got to know Sis. Although the Johnsons knew I had approval to visit with Sis, they seemed adamant that I not spend much time with her. I never did learn why this was so, but I always thought it might have been because Sis owned a valuable river farm next to the school's own farm and that perhaps Sis at some point had refused to donate the land or sell it to the school.

The farm land owned by the Buckhorn Association was immense, thanks to financing from Mr. Underwood. The farm was meant to support the school from proceeds of its crops and animals. But even more, the farm was meant to serve as a model to area residents for instruction in modern methods in agriculture. As such, each student who lived at school obviously was also going to be involved in the farm.

In 1945, Dr. Gabbard sent to Alice Cobb at the Pine Mountain Settlement School, an institution with similar purposes as Witherspoon, a brochure that had been in use since the 30's to advertise Witherspoon College. In the brochure, Dr. Gabbard noted that the few acres on which the first cabin was built for the school had grown to a good sized tract—a campus of 15 acres for school itself and total holdings of approximately 1,100 acres for the farm. Crops and orchards were planted to supply the school tables. Cattle and hogs were obtained—the best stock available—and from these the farmers of the section were able to improve their livestock. Through the school's agricultural program outreach, knowledge of improved methods of fertilizing and of cultivation was spread. The brochure noted the desire for better homes was leading to the building of improved dwellings. It was reported that one room cabins used by families for whom Witherspoon was intended to serve were giving way to more attractive and sanitary buildings. Up my holler, we had not gotten this news.

By the 1930's when Dr. Gabbard assumed leadership of the school, the campus for the most part was complete. New buildings were not a goal. Instead, the greater need was to improve and make warm and useful the buildings already in existence. Examples of this included an industrial arts department to teach auto-mechanics, carpentry, blacksmithing, and various trades. Again, high grade Jersey cows were a high priority. A horse for the use of the nurse, minister, and other workers was an immediate need. And high on the list also was a one-horse wagon for the farm, including harnesses for the mules. Other pressing needs listed by Dr. Gabbard that year included the following: books for the library, two sewing machines, two coal ranges for the Domestic Science building and for Worthington House, $1,000 to complete the new kitchen, and $800 for a state-of-the-art sound movie projector. These needs are interesting because they indicate the interests and direction that Dr. Gabbard saw for the future of the program when he took over the administration of the school.

During the 40's, significant improvements to the farm were noted. Dr. Gabbard reported to the New York benefactors that a specialist from the University of Tennessee, George Ellis, had taken over the management of the farm. During this period the trench silo was added to the barn, likely the first ever in Eastern Kentucky. People came from all around to observe this addition, with many expressing fear that the ensilage would heat and blow up the silo. More additions were made to the prized herd of Jersey cows. The basement of Lafayette Hall had been cleared out and a farm shop added to the instructional program in agriculture. The library at Albertson Hall now included a special section on vocational literature. And Dr. John Gardner of the University of Kentucky was instrumental in procuring a canning outfit for the institution.

Dr. Gabbard also proposed to the New Yorkers that the farm be expanded even more. He used for support suggestions from the University of Kentucky and the State Department of Forestry that the school invest in a saw mill for cutting and marketing valuable lumber on farm land, the purchase of the "Anderson Farm" consisting of 350 acres with its valuable timber and coal, even more additions to the Jersey herd, and enlargement of the barn. All of these proposed expenditures totaled about $25,000, which would have increased the budget by 55%. The figures were too steep for the members of the Association, and the proposal was referred to a committee on management in Kentucky—evidently not to be dealt with by the Association in New York.

When I later learned all this history, my suspicion as to why it was not desired that I visit Sis increased. She had exactly the land the school desired as "greatly needed." To some, my visiting her was likely a tear to a scab on an old wound. Nevertheless, efforts continued to expand the land holdings; and even if the school tried but was unable to obtain Sis's property, the school did acquire the Anderson Farm. It definitely was a part of the farm operations when I entered the school in 1952.

Finances for the school continued to deteriorate. The Association budget income figures for the 1953 fiscal year, my first full year at Buckhorn, were $17,000 less than the receipts of the Association the previous year. Fortunately by now the Association was not the only support the school received. On the positive side, Dr. Gabbard reported gift funding of scholarships amounting to $150 each to help with the care of students who had no income to provide for their own support. My parent's payments of $10 per month seemed to be so little in terms of the school's budget, but evidently the payments went a long way to support my being a student at Buckhorn. Based on these figures, it also appears the value of all my work at Buckhorn must have been about $60 per year.

With no knowledge of any of this historical information, I simply found myself—although of my own making—having some big issues with loss (from Granny, from my parents, from my sister, and from my horse Jim and other pets), so it was natural that I would make contact with Sis McIntosh. When I visited her, she seemed as glad to see me as I did her. Sis lived by herself like my Granny. Her husband Asbury, known as Posh, was deceased, as was their only son Burt. He had died in his 20's from pneumonia, and I believe he was at the time of his death studying to become a physician or to become some other highly educated professional. Going to Sis's was a little like going to a museum. Her house was a little dark. There were pictures of her son and husband everywhere. Not one of these pictures had anyone smiling. The subjects of the photographs resembled the individuals in the famous painting *American Gothic*, but with a mountain style flavor. Things looked to me like they had been placed in a particular spot, and other than for an occasional dusting were never touched.

Despite this home full of gloominess, for some reason Sis took a liking to me. She was very religious, as was I; and her past associations with Martha Gabbard gave us something in common to talk about. She let me look at some of her son's text books, the content of which was way over my head. I think I must have been one of the few visitors she had, and I often volunteered to help her with her chores. She made an impact on me I know because I wrote to Granny about her. The only personal effect I have left of Granny is a letter back to me in which she passed her blessing on Sis and even suggested that Sis and I hit the road for missionary work. Certainly we would have attracted a crowd had we done so. If Old Maude had been available, the crowds would have been even larger. In that same letter Granny sent to recommend a mission for Sis and me, she also included a dollar. For her to do so, Granny was definitely stretching her finances. Her total income, other than money she received for shipping cream and some occasional gift from one of her children, amounted to just three dollars a month from her old age pension.

What I soon learned the hard way was that one evening

I violated a strong rule not ever to be broken at Buckhorn. When I returned from my visit to Sis's, a few minutes later than I should have, the Johnsons came down hard on me. Mr. Johnson announced that I was "campused" for two weeks, which meant I was confined to my room immediately after dinner every day of the week and all day on Saturday and Sunday. I was still allowed to work on the farm, of course, and to go to Church.

Though hurt, what could I say or do? I went quietly to my room and resolved to try to do better in the future. As it turned out, being campused was not a great change in routine for me. Normal dormitory rules required all lights be off no later than nine in the evening, and we were to be in bed without any talking. Late at night, Mrs. Johnson often walked around the hillside behind the building to ensure that we followed the rules. She knew every boy by sight and sound. If she heard us whispering, she called us down by name from outside the window. If she did this, we stopped talking immediately and held our breath until she moved on.

There were other things about dormitory life I quickly learned—none of which made me excited about having left home. Mrs. Johnson came to the foot of the stairs every morning at six and roll-called every name as a wake-up. By the tone of her voice, we knew immediately our status with her. When she called a name, we needed to answer immediately, and alertly. A second call meant trouble. If she had to ascend the stairs to get an answer, her presence was equivalent to the Second Coming. Because the Johnson's son was the basketball coach at Buckhorn, an extra minute or two of sleep for the players could always be excused. Her voice softened when she called them by name.

As a part of this routine, we were also expected to get dressed and have our rooms clean and ready for inspection which took place while we were at breakfast. If Mrs. Johnson did not like what she saw, she took all our bedding and everything we had on our desks, in our dresser drawers, and in our closets and piled all of our belongings into the middle of the floor. She only did this once to me during my four years there, and I think that time may have been by accident because I believe she was really going after one of my roommates whom she did this to on a weekly basis. Or perhaps I had crossed her in some other way. Punishments were rarely explained.

Another dormitory life experience had to do with cleaning the bathrooms. Each student was assigned a rotation for cleaning these rooms for a week—except for the basketball players, who evidently had to avoid anything that might affect their shooting accuracy. The water in our dormitory was full of iron due to the plumbing that had been used in construction. The water both tasted and smelled like rotten eggs. In addition, the rust turned the enameled walls of the showers orange-red. On the first day I was assigned to clean the bathrooms, I learned that a scrubbing with Ajax would take off the rust. So as was my nature, I worked feverishly until by the end of the week, the fixtures were as white as when they were new.

Little was said about this until our regular Monday evening assembly. Mr. Johnson presided over these meetings; and on this occasion, he spent at least five minutes citing my work as an example to the other boys and setting a new standard for bathroom care. Not only was I embarrassed, I am certain I would not have received one vote had I been running for political office. I was blamed for everybody else's misfortune and derided for trying to be a "brown nose." Since I felt all of this was undeserved but having no way to either explain what happened or to get back in their good graces, I resolved to not respond to their taunts at all but just to look them directly in the eye and say nothing.

I also learned that I was to be treated differently than others in the dormitory because I was a paying student. On Fridays, all of the boys but me were told to bring down their sheets and dirty laundry. It was then bagged and sent out for washing. At the Monday assembly, each boy was given his return of clean linen and clothes. I, on the other hand, had to do my own laundry. My mother somehow or other got me a wash board, clothes pins, and an electric iron. We did not have electric at home, so the only thing available there were flat irons—which, of course, I had no way of heating without fire. Through my experience of doing my own laundry, I gained an insight to Mrs. Johnson. She talked tough and she was tough; but underneath that rough exterior, she had a heart of gold. In her own brusque way, she showed me how to iron shirts efficiently: first the collar, then the sleeves, the yolk, and finally the body. If you did as she showed you, you did not mess up any part of the shirt you had already worked on. Sometimes she slipped and even said, "That's a good job" to me. I never acknowledged her compliment because I knew if I did she would not give me another. Getting Mrs. Johnson's approval on my laundry skills was my first hint of success at Buckhorn.

My self-reliance led to Mrs. Johnson sometimes sending me over in town to the post office to retrieve the mail for the dormitory. This was a real treat because it gave me a heads-up on knowing whether or not there might be a letter from my mother or from Granny. That only happened occasionally, but getting a letter from home was the thing I anticipated more than anything else. Mrs. Johnson likely knew this, and this was her secretive way of showing me how much she cared.

As the weeks of my summer work passed, I experienced most aspects of farm life advertised by the school. We were assigned in groups to gather beans for canning, we fed the animals, and we bailed hay. Of particular interest to me, we also helped with cane when it came time to make molasses. This was a job my mother had talked about at home because her father was much sought after for his skills in making molasses. The juice to make molasses came from the stalks of cane run through a press powered by a mule who did nothing all day but move in a circle slowly pulling the arm that ran the press. The juice was then placed in a large metal pan filled by many sides like a maze and heated by a fire underneath the pan. The molasses maker stirred the juice with a skimmer to keep the molasses in a slow but constant motion and moving through the maze as the juice cooked over a steady fire for several hours. The green foam that formed during the cooking had to be removed from the pan. Making molasses is an art. If the fire is too hot, the juice will scorch. If the juice is not kept in motion, it will scorch. If it is cooked it too long, the juice will darken and turn bitter. But if the juice is not kept hot enough or cooked long enough, the molasses will be no good. The man who made molasses at Buckhorn was friendly but not very talkative. He had to attend to his work. If a person wanted to learn how to make molasses from him, one needed to learn from watching—not from being told how to do so. Based on my mother's evaluation, the molasses at Buckhorn were good. The maker's work supplied the kitchen for the entire winter. A favorite evening meal from that kitchen was a plate of molasses that had been mixed with baking soda. This frothy sweet foam, I later read in a story by Charles Dickens, was called treacle. The molasses explosion was served over two biscuits, which everybody prayed had not been burnt by the girls who did the cooking. When served, we all got a huge plate of mostly hot air.

The cane fields were more work for us than just making molasses. The renowned silo also had to be filled. To make the "ensilage," the cane was cut, chopped, and powered into the top of the silo. Another work committee, which included my membership, was assigned to stand in the silo and occasionally add water to the stuff flying down on us from overhead. We also were kept busy stomping the cane to help it compress so it would not rot. We had to keep moving to avoid being buried along with cane, which would have been a sweet but unwelcome way to die. At the end of the day, we spent a long time washing out all the flyings from our hair. I was most impressed with these modern agriculture methods. Making molasses and ensilage was more fun than work. It was different from anything I had ever done on our farm at home.

At this point, I fortunately never mentioned my skills in milking. But I did help take care of the chickens, a job that later merits its own revelations.

About the only real thing to do for fun after work was to occasionally visit the Crit Keen store across the street from our dormitory. If one got there at the right time of the day, one could be sure to hear a broadcast of a Cincinnati Reds baseball game, as Mr. Keen was a devoted fan. Also, if a boy had any money he could splurge with a moon pie and an Ale Eight. I rarely had any money, but I was a rabid fan of the Reds. I knew a lot about the team, because when the battery to our radio had any juice in it, my father often made up a reason for me to go to the house and bring back some drinking water—all the time knowing I would also report back on the score. I knew the players backwards and forwards, and nothing brought more excitement than a long pause from broadcaster Wait Hoyt's waiting for information to come in on the ticker and learning that Ted Klewzewski had hit a homerun into the laundry across the street from Crosley Field or into that mysterious place Wait called Burgerville. I knew the games were sponsored by Burger Beer, but it never dawned on me that Burgerville was a place made up simply to associate the beer with homeruns.

Later, when I finally actually got to Crosley Field, I was sorely disappointed to find there was no such place. I can assure you it existed in my head. The people in the town that I envisioned were not exactly on their way to a Mensa meeting; but wherever they were heading, they had to be careful and constantly watch the sky to avoid being hit on the head from an unexpected flying baseball.

Mr. Keen must have noticed that I rarely had money for a treat, or perhaps he was impressed with my interest and knowledge of the Reds. He was a quiet and generous man, as was his wife Osha. One day out of the blue he offered me a job. The furnace of the Keen home was fired by slack coal. Because the Keens did not want dust in the house from coal being dumped in the basement, I was offered the job of carrying in the coal, bucket by bucket. For this work, Mr. Keen proposed to pay me twenty-five cents an hour. This seemed like a fortune to me, so I immediately took him up on his offer.

Though no dust flew from my buckets, some of it did end up on me. At the end of my work, I often resembled a young coal miner. But that was no worry. It all washed off.

Later, Mr. Keen said due to my good work, he wondered if I might like to come over for a visit to watch television. This was almost too much for me to believe. Though I had heard of television from my cousin Benny Paul when he came to visit from Ohio, I had never seen it. Benny always came up with some new invention or novel way for us to make life easier or more fun when he came down, so I never thought too much about this new medium. Hardly anyone else in Buckhorn had seen television either. Mr. Keen and Dr. Gabbard had the only sets in town. They each had copper lines that ran to their shared antenna on top of the hill behind their homes from which they picked up three different stations.

First, to avoid a repeat of my debacle of visiting Sis McIntosh,

I made sure that I cleared visiting the Keens with the Johnsons before going over. Even if they had wanted to keep me from doing so, they were not likely to turn me down on this one. The Keens were a fixture at Buckhorn. I later learned that Crit and Osha had both attended Buckhorn themselves around 1914. Osha later transferred to another school, but Crit completed the Witherspoon program. They later learned that a man named Reynolds was looking to sell his store and his rights to being postmaster. So Mr. Keen and his brother bought out the store. Crit and Osha loaded up their possessions and floated them down the river from Leslie County to begin their new venture.

The Keens were told everything was free and clear when they bought the store, but they soon found out several loans were still outstanding against the property. Osha wrote letters to all the lenders to ask for time to pay, and a reprieve was given to them. They also learned the rights to the post office were being given to Reynolds who opened a new store in competition with them.

Despite this rough beginning, the Keens made ends meet by growing their own vegetables in their garden, living frugally, and making an honest dollar from running the store. Over the years, the Keens prospered enough to send four children through college. Evidently, the Keens also rewarded their children with material goods when appropriate. According to their daughter Jean, she and her older brother Quentin were once sent to Lexington to purchase a piano for her because of her love and skill with music. They returned with a Grand that cost twice as much as they had been authorized to pay for the instrument. The parents said nothing but endured the costs. It turned out to be a good buy. The piano still sits in the living room of the Keen home where Jean can sometimes be persuaded to play.

I have inquired about the unusual names of Crit and Osha Keen. I was excited to learn that Crit was named after a famous Governor of Kentucky, John J. Crittenden, who tried to prevent a break-up of the union prior to the Civil War. He opposed Andrew Jackson, the father of the modern Democratic party, and served as Attorney General under Millard Fillmore. In other words, Crit Keen was a Republican, though not an outspoken one. Osha's name, however, is more of a mystery. Her mother seemed to be partial to geography when naming her daughters—one was named Atlanta and another Erie—so perhaps she had some place in mind when Osha came along; but if so, she never identified the place. (Could it have been the ocean?)

The Keen store was not only a gathering place for students at Buckhorn, it was also the place one could find almost anything. If some part was needed on the farm, you went to Mr. Keen's store to get it; and Mr. Keen put the charge on the school's running account.

I recall once being sent to Mr. Keen's to get a few of "the largest nails he had."

"Alex, you do not want my largest nail," Mr. Keen told me.

"Why?" I asked. "That is what they sent me here to get."

"But I am sure that is not what they want," he replied and added, "Look, this is my biggest nail." It was as big as a railroad spike, and I wondered what use it could possibly have. When I saw the nail, I agreed. I then told Mr. Keen the use for which the nail was intended, and he guided me to one the proper size.

While surely Mr. Keen cleared some profit from his sales to the school, he also must have saved the school thousands of dollars. Basically, his store served as the school's parts depot. The school got what it needed when it needed it and rarely had to keep much inventory itself.

With this connection, the Johnsons quickly agreed to my visit, which turned out to be a weekly privilege. Three shows were an almost open invitation for me to spend time at the Keen home: *Your Lucky Strike Hit Parade, This Is Your Life*, and the quiz show *Twenty-one*. We were amazed at watching the stars of the Hit Parade—Snooky Lanson, Gisele MacKenzie, Russell Arms, and Dorothy Collins. Every week they came up with some new way to act out a top song. Later when the Diamonds' song, *Little Darlin'* stayed on the hit parade for 26 weeks, the cast was sorely tested; but somehow they kept their skits different from the previous week. (The song never made it to number one but was number two for eight straight weeks the year after I left Buckhorn.) For *Twenty-One*, I think I perspired as much as Charles Van Doren did when he was placed in the isolation booth and the host presented him with ungodly difficult questions. Only many years later did I discover my perspiration was real, while he was just acting.

We were startled and amazed when we tuned in the show *This Is Your Life* on December 7, 1955, to see someone from our area featured. It was Alice Lloyd, who had started Caney Creek Junior College in much the same way as Witherspoon College was envisioned. Like Dr. Murdoch, the finances for the school came from donations from East Coast states. I was proud to hear that Alice named her Caney Creek home Pippa Passes after a poem written by someone with the same last name as mine, Robert Browning, though at the time I had never heard of him. During the program we learned the school did not charge tuition; but like Buckhorn, everybody had to work. We also learned the rules were even stricter than those imposed on us: For the girls, the rules meant no jewelry, no cosmetics, no slang, and no high-heeled shoes. For the boys, there was to be no tobacco, no gambling, no liquor, no guns, and no unauthorized meetings with the opposite sex. After the show, money came pouring in, almost $250,000.

I have learned since that Alice Lloyd lived to be a hundred. The school's program has expanded to make it a four year college, and the name has been changed to honor its founder and is now known as Alice Lloyd College.

Mr. Keen's observational skills fit his given name. He never interfered with anything going on at Buckhorn, but he perhaps knew better than anyone else what was really happening. His sources of information were his own eyes and ears because he had an excellent view of the campus; and all he had to do was listen to the idle chatter of the students who congregated on his store front porch.

Why Crit and Osha Keen singled me out for their generosity and attention, I have no clue. No thought ever comes to me of Buckhorn without their names creeping in. They provided comfort to me when little was available from anywhere else. And they did it without telling anybody or expecting anything in return. That was their nature.

CHAPTER 5

Latin Is a Dead Language

Teachers are primarily messengers of meaning. While the old adage of "Don't shoot the messenger" certainly applies to most teachers, every now and then a symbolic shooting could be defended. At Buckhorn, there were teachers of both kinds: those who inspired and are memorable for their hard work, and a few who might have qualified for some career counseling on their own. With the passing of years, it becomes difficult to recall the source of what has been learned. The learning just becomes a part of us, and credit cannot be assigned. Then again, there are some teachers we are sure to remember whether or not we learned a lick from them.

What I can say about this is that in late August of 1952, the school bells rang; and all of us quickly picked up our schedules and situated ourselves at our desks. In my class there were more than sixty ninth-graders, most of whom came in from the feeder communities of Chavies, Krypton, Gays Creek, Bowlingtown (later to disappear from flooding by backwater when the Buckhorn dam was built), and from Buckhorn itself. Though only in one or two of my classes, two students in school I believe were returning soldiers from the Korean conflict, Franklin Gay and Garfield Sandlin, and were at least in their mid-twenties. One I believe not only was a student, but also drove a school bus. Having just turned thirteen, I likely was the youngest in my class. All of us were highly motivated, though for different reasons. Perhaps the most beautiful girl in class with her striking blonde curls and bright eyes showed much interest in me for all of one day; but I was too dumb to realize it and would not have returned any interest because I came for book learning, not for what probably motivated her most. At any rate, she moved on to more desirable prey the second day of school.

Rather than specifics of daily school life, my memories are more of the messengers who served as our teachers—some whose names today are no longer in my mind's record at all. Three teachers that first year, however, are indelibly inscribed there.

The first to come to mind, Clay Banks, taught vocational agriculture. The first class had hardly begun when someone raised a hand to ask Mr. Banks if he could be excused to go to the bathroom. Mr. Banks stopped class and addressed us by saying as adults we had arrived at the age that if we needed to use the facilities, we should just quietly leave the room, complete our duties, and return as quickly as possible so we would not miss any important information. Given this freedom, most of us were quite startled; but the year passed without one student ever abusing that freedom.

The second memory I have of Mr. Banks was his method of teaching. Each student was given a brown covered spiral notebook on which to record the material presented in class. Each day, a new topic was introduced that always began with "HOW . . . .," such as "How Maintain a Good Bloodline in Animals?" Being one to always challenge a messenger when presented with an opportunity, my hand quickly went up to ask if perhaps there might not be a better way to write this, as it just did not sound right grammatically. Mr. Banks defended his methodology by saying this was a class in agriculture, not English. That finished that subject.

Though few of us in class actually lived on a farm, the information imparted in Agriculture was more meaningful and stuck with us better than classes in biology, chemistry, physics, mathematics, or industrial arts because everything centered around something real and functional. For instance, learning the table of elements in chemistry was hard, but remembering *N, P,* and *K* was easy because we learned the right mix of nitrogen, potash, and potassium was critical for growing good crops. Those three chemical elements we learned for life.

Along with the agriculture class, Mr. Banks encouraged us to become members of the Future Farmers of America (FFA). Belonging to this organization provided us with the opportunity to either earn or purchase a blue jacket with Buckhorn embroidered on it. If a student did not make it to playing varsity basketball where he was rewarded with a team jacket, the FFA jacket was the second most-coveted thing worn in school. We further learned Robert's Rules of Order for conducting meetings and had contests to try to tie up somebody who wanted to get some idea put into action. Developing the skills of making, amending, or tabling a motion was essential, as well as rising to a point of order to object to what somebody proposed.

Coach Fred Johnson also stands out. Mr. Johnson was a very handsome person with prematurely gray hair, which I later learned was likely the result of his treatment during the time he was held as a prisoner of war during World II. He was our Civics teacher.

Although Mr. Johnson assigned us reading from the text book and gave tests over the material, he spent little time in class actually talking about the material he had assigned us to read. He was very big on our learning about the three branches of government—legislative, executive, and judicial. But mostly he spent the hour in philosophy, talking off the cuff about what is the right and wrong thing to do as we interact with each other. The branches of government have stuck with me as has the use of parliamentary procedure by senators and congressmen to try to promote or attack each other's proposals.

More important, I still grapple with the main point Mr. Johnson emphasized in class.

"It is not so important," he said, "where you set your individual bar for doing what is right."

"What is most important," he added, "is that wherever you set the bar—no matter how low—you must not go below that line."

I still am not sure I agree with Mr. Johnson, but I do have to say there have been many decisions in my life where when contemplating some action, I have asked myself if following through on what I was thinking of doing would be violating Mr. Johnson's guidance. So far, following his instruction has kept me honest, though on one occasion my refusal to cross that bar did cost me a job. Most of us in class liked what he said at the time because he seemed to be giving us a lot of room in regard to our own moral behavior. It should also be noted that in the years I was around Fred Johnson I felt he must have set a relatively high bar for himself.

Perhaps the most memorable teacher I encountered in my first year at Buckhorn was Mrs. Strode. She not only taught Latin, she was also in charge of the library. It was to the Albertson Library that we all moved from the main school building, Lafayette Hall, to learn that very important subject. None of us knew a thing about Latin, but we knew that if we ever planned to go on to college and become a "professional," we certainly should have the subject listed on our transcript. Scott Johnson, the head of our dormitory, must have done very well in Latin. He could recite verbatim much oratory from Greek and Roman poets and philosophers.

Mrs. Strode had three major duties at Buckhorn: teaching Latin, protecting the books in the library, and remembering where she was at any given minute. My time in her class lasted less than one of those minutes, perhaps a record that still stands for the completion of a course in high school.

In the library, we all sat at tables, rather than in individual desks. Our tables had trestles at the bottom to help keep them sturdy. When I sat down at my table, I unthoughtedly rested my feet on the trestle, which was a crime worse than damage to a federal building to Mrs. Strode, who obviously had never taken Civics under Mr. Johnson. Mrs. Strode did not direct me to move my feet. No, instead she approached me from behind, grabbed me by the ear, led me to the door and told me to never come back to the library again. At the time, I did not even know what I had done wrong.

I later learned that Mrs. Strode performed her duties at practically no cost to the school, being paid mainly by provision of her own room and board. I also learned that she had a rather high level of paranoia regarding the male sex. My roommate Bobby later told me that Clarence, he, and some other students frequently walked behind her when she locked up the library in the evening and returned to her living quarters. Today, we might call this stalking. But any formal charges would never have stuck, for Mrs. Strode was totally safe. The only intent of the boys was to feed her paranoia, and they were pretty good at it. No one would have laid a hand on her no matter what the opportunity. Whether Mrs. Strode erroneously thought of me as one of her stalkers or perhaps made some association with Jack the Ripper and me, I had to get a schedule change; and I never had Latin in high school. I believe dementia finally overcame her, and she finally left Buckhorn. I do know that if she was paid a dollar for her services, the school misspent its money.

Jean Keen recalls that Mrs. Strode frequently used an expression to describe any student she perceived to be hopeless. "That one is not to the manor born," she would exclaim. In my case, she was right about my heritage, but I still think she gave up on me a little early.

The teachers of English, General Mathematics, and General Science were so entertaining their names do not come to me anymore. The content of their subject matter also escapes me— with one exception. In English, we spent a great deal of time learning the Dewey Decimal System, so we could make full use of the library. Melvil Dewey, the inventor of the system, I learned, was a man after my own heart, perhaps for our common leaning toward an obsessive-compulsive disorder. I do believe Dewey's condition was much more severe than my own. For instance, as a youngster he totally reorganized his mother's pantry. Dewey also on one occasion scheduled dates with three different girls in the same evening and was precise enough to get to all of them on time. (I would have been lucky to just get one girl as a date at all.) In my own case, as a child I just graded recipes in my sister Joyce's home economics cookbook. The idea of classifying books by a decimal system came to Dewey during a dull sermon, where he obviously was concentrating on something other than the preacher's message. His story is evidence that some good after all can come from speaking described by John Witherspoon as "half way between sense and nonsense."

As we covered the subject in English class, a lot of good I thought this information was going to do for me—since I had been outlawed from the library building. Months later after my first contact with Mrs. Strode, however, I ventured back to the library. To my surprise, she had no memory of me— or much of anything else, I guess.

There was some irony in this event. When I finished my time at Buckhorn, Dr. Gabbard actually offered me the position of librarian at a salary of $15 per week. I do not know exactly how he could do that. Teachers, I learned by this time, were paid from the county public school program. The county, it appears, must have given Dr. Gabbard full authority on who was hired.

The library was thought of as an integral part of Witherspoon. It was named after Charles C. Albertson, unknown to me except for his rare book of poetry. Albertson Hall was the first public library in Perry County. Books to supply the library were always a high priority. The need was number seven on a list presented to the Buckhorn Association in the late 30's as follows: "Books of reference, biography, and fiction to modernize our library and keep it up to the requirements set forth by the Southern Association of Colleges and Secondary Schools." I wonder what the Southern Association would have thought about staffing the collection of books with a sixteen-year-old. I also wonder if Rossiter's *The Federalists Papers* could have been found in the reference section.

Personally, access to the library was a high hope of mine because books had always been so important to me. I actually read many books on subjects I was not assigned in class. This had always been the case with me, for books were hard to come by on Long Shoal. We had no library or any other reading material other than the Bible and the seasonal catalog from Montgomery Ward. One of my best memories is the lucky find of a wooden box in our church. The box contained many books sent from the Maysville Presbyterian Church. Many of the books were partially chewed away by mice that had used the box and its contents for nests. Because of their condition, Martha Gabbard told me I could take what I wanted—which was all of the books, including those with urine stains and gnawed pages. Many nights lying in front of the coal grate fire in our bedroom, I spent hours reading from *The Adventures of Tom Sawyer* and *Huckleberry Finn*. I read about King Arthur and The Knights of the Roundtable. I read *Black Beauty* and *Star* (another horse story). I read *Bruce, the War Dog*, where I learned about the fight of our World War II soldiers in the Pacific. My sister Mary says she read all of Shakespeare's plays before the third grade. Miss Violet Siebert who had offered to take me with her to Princeton also subscribed me to a book of the month club for a while, which was another source of reading for us.

This reading had been the greater part of my library until I got to Buckhorn. One other source of reading material fate brought to me. A neighbor woman near us lived in a beautiful two-story Victorian house with hand-carved gingerbread railings on her porches. The house was surrounded by a picket fence where dahlias blossomed with every color in the summer time. Meg Greer's house looked far too fancy to be up our holler. It was necessary to pass by her house going to and coming from school; and when passing, school children generally hurried their pace because Meg was not considered by many as very friendly.

But Meg's dahlias were like sirens to my sister and me; and one day as we stopped to sneak a closer look at them, Meg leaned over the fence and asked if we would like biscuit and jam sandwiches. It was my duty, being six years older than she, to insure Mary made it to and from school safely—which was not always a sure thing because Mary's walking pace was one she herself set without consultation with others and one which could not be changed by any outside persuasion. We frequently faced real dangers of copperhead snakes, high water in the creeks, or swarming wasps at certain times of the year. Mary has told me that when I left home to go to Buckhorn I was replaced as her safety patrol by our fox hound. She says our dog Bruce walked her to school every day, where he lay at her feet and growled at the teacher until Mother intervened. Even when he was banished from the school building, Bruce met Mary at the school door to walk her back home once he learned what time the day ended.

Although we were concerned that we might meet the same fate as intended for Hansel and Gretel and end up in the oven of Meg's wood burning stove, Mary, who was usually easily persuaded by any adventure I might propose, joined me to sit on Meg's front porch. There as we ate sandwiches we found stacks of *Time Magazine* on her chairs, most of which were well out of date. But old news was new news to us. We eagerly learned of the coronation of Queen Elizabeth, of President Truman's daughter Margaret's trauma from having her piano fall through the floor in the White House, and of Dwight Eisenhower's designs on becoming President. The reading material was current events to us, and the biscuit and jam took away our evening hunger to the point that Mother asked us if we were not feeling well.

Mary, who could tell the truth and still remain secure in knowing that by doing so she would not be shot, quickly blabbed that Meg had given us a treat. My father almost became unglued on learning of this. Meg and her husband Willie were not well thought of in the community—even though they professed to own hundreds of acres of good trees, which could be a source of cash for anyone who might enter into an agreement to cut the timber. They blocked every attempt at getting electricity up our way because they refused to let power poles cross their property. The road to our house followed the creek bed because they would not grant us a right of way to cut a road from the hillside. They had a well- deserved reputation as stingy people. Mainly, I thought their poor standing and the reason for my father's outrage was because they were Democrats.

My father, however, had a much different story to tell. He began with stories of whippings he had received from his father due to tales Meg Greer had told on him, tales my dad said were untrue. I can vouch that Dad could really stretch the truth for humor but not in conversation that was serious. I know there once was a time when he came home intoxicated and brought with him some chickens he said he had stolen from Meg. He said he did this to get even with her for the lies she had told on him when he was a child. He insisted that the chickens be cooked at once. At 2:30 in the morning, my mother went to the hen house and killed two of her own chickens and fried them. The next day, she returned Meg's chickens and told her what happened. Meg thanked my mother and sheepishly added, "I guess he never will forgive me, will he?"

In later years, my sister learned the divide between Meg and our family ran much deeper. It seems that brothers of my father's grandmother Rhoda (France) Hogan had left Lee County and settled as far away as Arkansas because of a run-in between themselves and Meg's relatives over something political that happened as far away as Jackson. When one of the brothers went to get the horses, a relative of Meg's started a fight with him. The brother defended himself with a knife. Later, in retaliation, Meg's relatives carried the fight further—this time with guns. In defending himself, one of my Dad's uncles shot dead one of Meg's ancestors. Though it was self-defense, all of the brothers were facing prosecution because not one of the brothers was going to tell who pulled the trigger. To avoid the legal outcome, all of the brothers left the county overnight.

Mary also discovered that beautiful house Mary and I had been so curious about had actually been built by the hands of my great-grandmother's family, including those who hurriedly left the territory. The house and much of the hundreds of acres of land around it was taken over by Meg's people by adverse possession. In later years, my grandmother Hallie (Hogan) Browning always said, "You know, they have no deed to that land." That house might have been in our family had it not been for this fracas.

One does not easily forget such an event, and my father though he did not tell us of this history did warn us to not get too close to Meg. But there were many more times she did offer us treats and let us read her magazines. We also were invited into the house where we saw an organ. I asked if she could play and learned she could. Knowing we had an organ in our little church but no one who could play it, I asked if she would ever consider doing so. She replied she did not think so. I later learned that Martha Gabbard had about the same opinion of Meg as my father. But, of course, Martha was not only Presbyterian which Meg was not; she was also a Republican, which likely accounted for some of those differences.

Nothing as exciting as a mountain feud kept me from reading during my first year at Buckhorn, though Mrs. Strode did. In spite of this difficulty, my academic year was busy and everything I had hoped high school would be. School days were the highlight of my life at that time, as indeed they always had been. My grades were good—very good it turned out.

Other aspects of my life that first year at Buckhorn had their highs and lows, but in the classroom, Buckhorn to me fulfilled entirely the goals Dr. Murdock and the Buckhorn Association had outlined in its Act of Incorporation: I learned some skills to help me in life, and no longer was I as "unchurched" as when I enrolled.

CHAPTER 6

Round Ball Mutiny

The early history of secondary education in Kentucky is a sorry one. Training at this level was not even mandated in the state's constitution until the early teens of the twentieth century, and then only one high school per the 120 counties of the state was required. Every year it seems Kentucky battled Mississippi for having the worst schools in the nation. This lack of good schools provided both the need and opportunity for independent and privately operated educational institutions such as Buckhorn to flourish. Even if Buckhorn only provided a high school education, the name Witherspoon College gave it more prestige.

By the 50's there were public schools all across the state; but in counties with large geographic areas and rough terrain, certainly one high school in each county could not possibly have been accessible for everyone in the territory. The larger cities and towns generally had the best schools because that is where the money, people, and interests were. Though there were high schools of all shapes and sizes throughout the rest of the area, Buckhorn and a dozen or more settlement schools still fulfilled a very useful service.

Wherever there were high schools, the game of basketball was sure to follow. It does not take a lot of youngsters to play the sport. It also in those days did not take a lot of money to operate a program. Thus basketball became *THE* sport for most schools.

Perhaps the most famous basketball team that proved this point was Carr Creek, the team that represented the 14th region in the state basketball tournament in 1928. Our Coach Johnson of our beloved Wildcats and our social studies teacher emphasized just two numbers in all his discussions in and out of class. As the social studies teacher, he made sure we knew we were in the 7th Congressional District—a position almost always held by a Democrat during my time at Buckhorn. The coach also always pushed the Wildcats for success in the regional tournament—the 14th—in order to make the trip to the "Sweet Sixteen" state championship play-offs.

The success of Carr Creek in 1928 was such that every other school no matter how small or poor was motivated and believed it could also rise to such an occasion. Carr Creek had no gym. The players also had no uniforms, and I have heard even no shoes until some benefactor from Eastern Kentucky State College bought some for them. Their outdoor court was on a "bench" (plateau) on a steep hill side with a creek below. A ground rule for playing at Carr Creek was that if the ball went over the hill during play, the last boy to shoot or touch the ball had to retrieve it. What greater motivation could a player have to hit every shot taken?

Despite these conditions, Carr Creek advanced to the finals of the state championship, where unfortunately they lost in five overtimes to the Ashland Tomcats by a final score of 13-11. Both teams were later invited to a national tournament held in Chicago. By then, Carr Creek had drawn statewide attention and support. They became Kentucky's team. Although it was not a national winner, the team gave such a good account of itself that on the return stop at Louisville via railroad, the owner of *The Courier Journal* arranged a huge banquet for the players.

Carr Creek actually did win the state title in 1956, the graduation year of my class. Their success proved any school could do it. It goes without saying that Buckhorn students sought to equal such success and were driven to be the best in the region. In truth, the odds were stacked against us. Records show that Hazard, an independent city school, has represented the 14th region twenty-one times in the state tournament. In our day Hazard had one of the best facilities in which to play and often hosted the regional tournament, giving it a home court advantage. Further, the school had more scouts than the New York Yankees. If a player anywhere around was good, it was likely the school would recruit him to play for the Bulldogs.

A dream of every youth even higher than being named a saint was the ultimate goal of playing college ball for The University of Kentucky Wildcats. This goal was more likely to be achieved if you played at Hazard because of better recruiting possibility. As opposed to current talent, in the 50's almost every player at U.K came from within the state. Compare that to the national champion team of 2012, where I believe not one of starting five actually grew up in Kentucky.

There were high school athletic association rules about playing within your school boundaries, but they were easily by-passed. In 1952-53, Hazard recruited a player named Johnny Cox, who not only led Hazard to the state championship, but afterwards led Kentucky to the national championship. Johnny really was from Letcher County and normally would have played for that school. He got to Hazard because his father suddenly found employment in Hazard and moved his family there. No one could blame Johnny for making such a move, but there was always heavy resentment toward Hazard and a lingering sense of unfairness for what happened. Hazard has named a street after Johnny, which shows how much care the inhabitants have for what other people might think.

The boundary for the Buckhorn School serves a remote geographic area of Perry County; but as a private boarding school, students came there from a six-county region along with a few from adjacent counties, such as was my case. In addition, the school had an old but very functional and well-maintained gymnasium. Buckhorn therefore was also in a good position to attract talent not only locally, but also from other areas.

From the time the Geer Gymnasium opened in 1924—dedicated by the Governor of the State—and up to 1953, the most acclaimed team to represent Buckhorn was that of my first year in school. During the season, statewide polls placed the Wildcats as high as eighth in the state. This team was put together by fate because the Perry County School system was undergoing badly needed construction and consolidation. Out went such names as Viper and Vicco High Schools, and in came names like Dilce Combs Memorial and M.C. Napier. Some very good basketball players were caught up in these changes and were quite unhappy about being separated from a team on which they expected to play. While Buckhorn did not have the facility and status of Hazard, it did have a very astute young coach. Coach Fred Johnson had just completed a successful first year at Buckhorn. As a follow-up, he aggressively went after these disgruntled players and convinced them to come as a group to play at Buckhorn.

The players' abilities and notoriety preceded them. Even before school began, the atmosphere of the community, the school, and especially the dormitory was at fever pitch. The change was quite a change from the hum drum of the summer work that occupied the time of us working on the farm until school began.

Just a few days before school started, the word was given that Coach Johnson would be holding try-outs for basketball. With the new talent moving in, hardly anyone expected to make varsity, but many had the fervent hope they could play junior varsity. Everyone, that is, but me. My game of interest was baseball and nothing else. In contrast, there were students in the local community who came to live in the dormitory for no other purpose than to see if the door to basketball would be opened to them. Two of them joined my roommate and me and filled up the four army bunk beds in our room. On the days before try-outs, more and more pressure came for me to go down to the gym to try to make the team. I finally consented, not because I expected to make the team, but just to see what could possibly cause such a commotion.

When we got there, Coach Johnson said very little to us. He simply threw out a lot of basketballs and told us to dribble around and shoot whatever shots we wanted. I was impressed to see that many basketballs, for the total Long Shoal Elementary inventory consisted of just one ball, which had been purchased from proceeds of a pie supper where my father had been the auctioneer. At that event, I proudly purchased for three dollars a chocolate pie made by Dora Fox, a girl who had my eye. When we tried to eat the pie, the filling was tasty. But the crust was tougher than a razor strap and ended any further interest I might have had in Dora.

Though not particularly motivated by Coach Johnson's orders, I did appreciate such loose direction. One reason I never really liked basketball was that I did not like someone guarding me with his hands in my face. Coach Johnson's first statements helped me avoid this drawback. When I got a ball, I immediately went to my accustomed place on the court, just over the mid stripe, to attempt a shot. I knew from experience that in most cases no one picked you up that far distance from

127

the goal and that I would be free to shoot. I planted my feet, aimed high and far with all my strength, and swish, the ball fell through the net. Thinking no one had seen me, I retrieved the ball and dribbled back to the position where I was comfortable. I shot again, and swish, the ball went through the net again. I was feeling pretty good about my success. I brought the ball out again and sank another shot, making it three in a row. (Though my talent was limited, my vision was extraordinary.) Out of the clouds from somewhere, Coach Johnson yelled "Browning, sit down!"

"Well, thank God, that's over," I thought as I found a seat on the bleachers. Later it finally dawned on me that I had made the first cut when Coach Johnson announced that anyone not sitting was excused from the gym. Sadly, one of those excused happened to be one of my new roommates who disappointedly soon moved from the dormitory. My heart went out to him because he wanted so badly to make the team.

My mourning period was not long, for a bigger concern for me was what next I could do. I did not want to play basketball. Fortunately, the problem soon resolved itself. The second day of practice Coach Johnson had us form two parallel lines. He then handed out balls with the directive that we were to pass across first to the player directly in front of us, then to his left, and then to his right. We were to do this as fast and hard as we could. Flying balls like cannon balls hit me in every part of my anatomy. On reflection, I have come to the conclusion that in a war zone, I might have done well as a sniper but would have been extinguished very quickly in hand-to-hand combat. Coach Johnson never said anything to me, but I am sure as he watched this exercise he was thinking that if I were to be on the team, he would not just be stuck with a "one man team," but perhaps with a "one play player."

When practice was over, I summoned the courage to talk

with the coach. I told him that though I truly enjoyed the sport, I really did not see myself playing for the basketball team. I asked him if there might be something else I could do to help out. His face actually showed an expression of relief because he no doubt read my pitiful look and perhaps saw a way out of having to tell me to leave the gym.

Evidently, my timing was also right, because I was told I could help out as a ball boy, a position for which no one had at that point even expressed an interest. Perhaps no other student at Buckhorn would have returned to the dormitory with the feeling of success I had—not making the team, but being named to the position of ball boy.

The next day the new recruits to the team settled into the room right next door to mine. I was thirteen and skinny. In contrast, these guys looked super human to me. Despite their size and stature, I found all of them to be great people to be around. Over the time they spent at Buckhorn, they befriended me more than once. They teased me a lot but always in good humor. I think I got to know them as well as anybody in the school. Each had his own individualism that sticks in my mind even today. Eli Feltner, the oldest and definitely the player the team looked to for points, was more serious-minded and purposeful in what he did. I think of him as the "Wise Old Judge" of the group.

Frosty Napier was the tallest and most rugged. His nickname was right; for when he got hot, it showed first in his ruddy face. When one looked at Frosty, the word that came to mind was "rough." And "rough" was his role on the team. If the Wildcats needed a rebound or a player moved out of the way for someone on our team to get a shot away, it was Frosty who got the job. Not always recognized, there was a sensitive side to him. Frosty had an underlying depth of soul that showed only when he sang. And he was very good at singing just for himself. When he put sound to the Hilltopper's *"P.S. I Love You,"* the song sounded just like it was written to be—a letter to someone very special. Frosty could also frequently be heard singing *"See the pyramids along the Nile, Watch the sun rise on a tropic isle. . . . Fly the ocean in a silver plane; See the Jungle when it's wet with rain. . . ."* words from Jo Stafford's *"You Belong to Me."* When Frosty sang, he always appeared to have his mind far away from where life had placed him.

Cliff Barker was probably the "teen idol" in the group and no doubt a favorite of the girls. Without being vain, he was always careful as to his dress and grooming. And that is the way he played basketball, with timing and precision.

Arnold Brewer, nicknamed "Bear" was the most out-going of the group and could have served as the team's social secretary. One could not be around him without laughing. He sometimes routed Mr. Johnson's weekly assembly meetings with some outrageous remark. Once when I had been driven almost to tears over something, Arnold approached me and asked, "What's wrong with you, Chief Rain-In-The-Face?" That was the last time I think I ever showed that expression again in my years at Buckhorn. By his words, Arnold had given me an exalted position for which crying was incongruent.

When these players were joined by home-grown players such as Clarence Helton and Bobby Edwards, the 1952-53 Buckhorn Wildcats made a formidable foe to literally every school in our whole area. As a naïve sojourner, they were my heroes, as they were to most every other student in school.

Believe it or not, as the basketball season wore on, my own status improved along with the team's success. Mr. Johnson used my services and upgraded my title to "Equipment Manager." As such, I had the key to the room that held the equipment and uniforms. If a player needed new socks, new shoes, or ace bandages, the player got it on authorization from the coach and then only by checking it out through me. Coach Johnson also gave me the job of official scorer for the team, which ultimately led to my highest achievement. Once in a game an opposing player entered the game without checking in at the official scorer's table. I reported this to the referee, who promptly called a technical. Our player made the free throw, and we also got the ball back. In the end, we won the game by one point, just the difference caused by that technical. Without even touching the ball, I had made the difference in the final score.

I also was assigned the role of calling in the results of the game to the local radio station and the *Hazard Herald*. If I felt some player had made a crucial play or scored a significant goal, this also got reported. Totally unplanned, I became the unofficial press agent for the team. There were times I even ventured to offer my opinion on the play of a particular player to Coach Johnson. For example, if someone had not done well at the free throw line, I reported his game percentage. When this happened, the player spent extra time in practice on skill development and going through the motions required to improve accuracy.

The job of scorer-manager was one I kept throughout my years at Buckhorn. The chief advantage of the position to me was that I got to go to every game. For anyone not on the team in some capacity or as a cheerleader, there were plenty of times this was not possible. No activity buses went to games; and even if there were, most of the feeder communities were too far for the students to return to school in the evening to ride a bus to a game.

These trips were my first opportunity to see what the real Eastern Kentucky was like. I vividly recall the gym at Kingdom Come. At each end of their gym were floor to rafter rock walls housing open fire places. To these walls were attached the basketball goals. Lighting for the gym was provided by 100 watt light bulbs hanging by long cords from the rafters. While primitive, at least the school had a gym. But if a player slid out of bounds under the goal, he might look like Cinderella's brother when he got back into the game.

One of these trips stands out. It was to a game at Hazard after which a heavy snow storm hit the area. To return to campus we had to head up a mountain with three switch backs on the road. My memory is the mountain was known as First Mountain, and a folk lore story about it was that a hitchhiker at one time flagged down the same car three times. Going down the mountain was treacherous at any time. Going up the mountain in a snow storm was almost suicidal. I recall that after we were about half way up during one heavy snow, the bus started sliding to the edge of the road. Coach Johnson called for all of us to get off the bus. All passengers then pushed the vehicle the rest of the way up the hill while the driver hung on for dear life to steer the vehicle away from the sharp drop off to nowhere.

The other reward I sometimes received was on some occasions I was able to spend the night with my Aunt Georgia who lived in Hazard. Her husband owned a taxi service known as Igo, after his last name. (His advertising slogan was "I Go, You Go, We all go, Igo.") In an effort to see if any historical reference exists of the company, I have found none. However, I did find a note on his son Bud. Internet comments listed information about the old Hazard airport. One person commented, "Well, Bud Igo crashed his plane behind the Grand-Vue Drive Inn. . . . Came to rest in Kenneth Zimmerman's back yard." (Bud later flew the personal plane of Governor Louie Nunn, who as one might guess was a Republican.) Bud was a dare devil. Once he crashed his motorcycle and lost all of his early memory. Nothing was more delightful to him than coming to Granny's and listening to her recite stories from his early life, which was all new to him. (After my Buckhorn years, Bud picked me up in his plane and flew me to Hazard the day of his mother's funeral. On the way, he did double sideways summer saults with the plane. He thought he had scared me, but I startled him when I asked if he could roll it again. When we landed, the plane stopped just a few feet from the side of the mountain. The Hazard airport was noted for its short runway.)

The basketball teams that followed the 52-53 school year were perhaps not as talented, but they were still very competitive. Coach Johnson used the success of the mutineer team to schedule Clark County in Winchester and Lafayette High School in Lexington the next year, which provided the first trip out of the mountains for most of us. We even stayed overnight in a hotel. Most players on that team were also dormitory students. The shooting star was Bige Combs, who reminded me of my own approach to scoring. Bige was famous for his long shot from the outside with arches so high one could have had time to read a book before the ball came down, that is, if Mrs. Strode had let the book be checked out from the library. It seems that Coach Johnson had also remained active in recruiting. Joining the Wildcats from across the hill in Breathitt County were Curly Smith, his younger brother, and Bill Turner. Bobby Edwards was a returning player from the previous year.

In modeling the strategy of the famous University of Kentucky Coach Adolph Rupp, the style of play for most high schools in the 50's was aggressive man-to-man and sometimes a game-long full-court press. But Coach Johnson did work in some zone defense and taught some plays to break a zone if used by an opponent.

I have always felt Buckhorn was the only team in history to actually have two zone defenses, one carefully taught, and the other learned by instinct. The reason I say this was that our gym was located in the flood plain. The biggest flood in the area is historically referenced in 1937, but similar devastations hit the campus the year before I went to Buckhorn and a year after I left. The results of this repeated flooding caused the playing floor to have dead spots. If opponents could be forced to dribble over one of these spots, surprising bounces occurred—often sideways and away from the dribbler. With no time to react, the opponent could only stand there with his mouth open and watch one of our players intercept the ball and run in for a score. Likely this is where the real estate slogan of "location, location, location" came from. I cannot vouch that teams were zoned to force them into these precarious places. But I do know that our players knew where many of dead spots were and carefully avoided them as they brought the ball up the court. I am confident that if the regional finals had been held in the Buckhorn gymnasium, the Wildcats would have been on their way to the state tournament.

Harvey Murdoch, in founding Buckhorn, would certainly have approved the spirit of the play of the Wildcats in the early 50's. Though later teams from Buckhorn actually went farther in tournament play—winning the regionals in '88 and '89—none received more accolades than the mutineers who came to Buckhorn for the '52-53 season. One can be sure that no coach ever in a team meeting used Mr. Murdoch's favorite admonition of "Press Them Severely." It is for certain, however, that Coach Johnson's teams did just that in every game they played.

CHAPTER 7

The Psychology of Chickens

As the end of my first summer at Buckhorn drew near, the anticipation of our year-long work assignments grew among those of us set to earn our keep. We quickly learned the advertised idea of a fifteen-hour schedule meant little for most duties. True, some jobs would require crews working for a set time each day. But most duties meant spending the time necessary—whether it was for two hours on one day or much more than that on others.

No one ever gave reason, but my job was to take care of the chickens, which was my job for every day of the week for whatever hours were required. I could not have been more pleased.

I learned that Buckhorn had been in and out of the poultry business since at least the late 1930's; and as a part of its "modern-day agriculture" intent, the school used all the best techniques for egg production. A poultry specialist from the University of Kentucky even showed workers how to prevent egg loss by debeaking the hens. The chickens of choice were New Hampshire Reds, and at one time the flock numbered more than 600. They were raised with care by the work boys spanning from the time the chickens were in the school's four brooders to the time they were sent to market. By the time I arrived at the school, the chicken house had been relocated high on the hill near Worthington Hall, the home of the "little girls."

The reason I was so happy with my assignment is I had a long and intensive history with chickens before I came to Buckhorn. That history began one day while I was riding behind Granny to the store. We stopped off to visit with her good friend, Georgia Palmer, the person who held Sunday school for the Crawford families. One of Georgia's hens had a new hatching of young chicks which intrigued me greatly. On our way back from the store, Georgia stopped us and delivered two of the baby doodles to me as my very own. One was jet black, which I named Georgia. The other was snow white, which I named Nazzi after Georgia's next door neighbor. Unfortunately, Nazzi did not thrive and died within two days.

Georgia, on the other hand, quickly became my best friend. She followed me everywhere, ate out of my hand, and actually seemed to enjoy being held. A characteristic I evidently share with many others is to personify my pets, that is, assign human qualities to them. This was pointed out to me by one of my psychology teachers when I went off to college. Some discussion in class triggered my experience with Georgia. The teacher explained that Georgia's behavior was a clear example of simple imprinting. I conceded the teacher's point, but I firmly believe that if there were a Mensa Society for chickens, Georgia could have been a charter member due to her giftedness.

In support of my teacher's position, I also agree with the old truism, "As the twig is bent, the tree is inclined to grow," and that my care of Georgia made her different from other chickens. Georgia also serves as a good example of the ongoing debate over "Nature vs. Nurturance" in terms of what we end up being in life, whether we end up a criminal or a saint. I do know that even though at the time I had not previously engaged in the unanswerable debate of which is more important in shaping our lives—nurturance or nature, I was committed to provide the best care I could to the chickens assigned to me at Buckhorn. I aimed to turn out the smartest chickens in Perry County. And it must be said that if I had succeeded with the red hens as well as I had done with my black one, I might have become locally famous.

To illustrate this, consider the life of Georgia. She rode in the back of the truck with us when our family moved to Ohio from Kentucky and later again made the trip with us when we moved back. She even provided the gift of an egg to us on one of the trips. Georgia was a "Free Chicken" and went where she wanted, even into our house if she felt like it. On these visits, Georgia always used the best toilet behavior and never once had an accident. Many times my mother would be occupying herself with her kitchen duties only to be startled by a surprise visit by Georgia. "Well, hello there, Miss Georgia, how are you today?" my mother asked. Georgia clucked incessantly as she came up to Mother, apparently gossiping about her neighbors. Then as suddenly as Georgia came into the house and after dutifully having reported the news, she left and went about her daily business.

Our dogs occasionally chased the other chickens, but they understood that Georgia was never to be teased. An on-going danger where we lived was for the chickens to be devoured by foxes. Georgia, however, outsmarted them all. The only real problem she ever had was psychological. One year we put duck eggs under her when she was "setting." She accepted the baby ducks as her own. However, as was their nature, when she guided her babies too close to the creek, the ducks walked into the water and did what ducks do—swim. Georgia was apoplectic. She raced up and down the banks clucking to them to please get out of the water. They finally did. After that, Georgia avoided the creek.

As a psychologist, I have generalized human behavior from this experience. I have learned that parents may be somewhat accepting of some differences in their children, but behavior too much out of the range of expectancy for a family can often lead to all kinds of distress—for the parent as well as the child. In many cases, the parents blame themselves and ask where they went wrong. In other cases, they reject the child along with the behavior and often with disastrous results. At least in Georgia's case, she loved her ducks as much as her chicks. She cared for them all until they were old enough to go their own way.

Georgia lived to a ripe old age. As the end came near, she became very feeble and walked with a tilt. Then she started crowing, a very unnerving thing from a hen. In our family this was considered bad luck. My father quoted an old saying that was not old or familiar at all to my sister and me, for we had never heard a hen crow. Father said we would have to kill Georgia and recited the saying to support his judgment:

> "A whistling woman and a crowing hen
> will surely come to no good end."

Thankfully, I was at Buckhorn and did not have to hear this pronouncement. But my sister did. To protect Georgia, she placed her in a box to sleep beside her bed. She even propped her up so that she did not fall over. On the second day, Georgia died peacefully in her sleep. She received a proper burial. This wonderful friend was with us for about ten years. We later learned that a chicken, if it has a good life and is allowed to live out its normal days, will sometimes live about seven years. But how many chickens do any of us know actually get the chance to die from natural causes?

Again, with this experience, I did not see my work assignment as work at all. I faithfully walked up the hill each morning to feed and water the chickens—more than I had ever seen in a group at one time. One bother I had was they all looked alike, so I was unable to identify them individually. I also went back in the evening to gather the eggs, do clean-up work, and get them situated for the evening. My reputation was such that more than fifty years later on talking with another boy who attended Buckhorn at the same time as I did, he commented, "Oh, I remember you. You were the chicken boy!"

Yes, I was. And I was quite proud of having that title. As the year progressed, my duties changed. Once a year, the school ordered a new supply of chickens. As what should have been a clue that the better days for modern agriculture at Buckhorn had passed, we were down to two brooders. And they both had electrical shorts in them, which could cause them to fail at any moment. This meant that someone had to be present every night to be sure the brooders did not short out and the chickens die from over exposure. So my additional duties required that I sleep with the 200 chicks to insure they kept warm. The timing of the purchase of the chicks was to have them laying during the following holiday season before they molted, stopped laying, and were sent to chicken heaven. The Buckhorn hens were not told of this, but an unwritten rule of life for chickens is "Lay or Die." Today, this has become an exact science. Most chickens live their lives in cages, and daily records will identify those to end up in the pot early. The Buckhorn chickens were somewhat luckier. Since they all looked alike and were kept in a flock, the non-producing hens could pass incognito. Most of them though did their duty, and I did mine.

Compliments poured my way as I delivered the dozens of eggs to the cafeteria each day. Things changed, however, the next summer when I returned from my stay at home.

An old problem with the chickens had re-occurred. Some of the hens had started eating their eggs. The school also had a new person in charge of farming, Mr. Brown. Though very sociable, Mr. Brown was not an expert in poultry from the University of Kentucky; and his training had not familiarized him with the art of debeaking. His solution instead was to have me beat the hens to their eggs by gathering the eggs more frequently. This was no problem for me until school began, though we did ponder the reason why a chicken would engage in cannibalism. Someone offered that the problem might be related to diet. Crushed oyster shells were bought, and sure enough the problem subsided for a time.

However, shortly after school began again, the chickens reverted to their old behavior. Mr. Brown instructed me to make the trip up the hill to gather the eggs at morning recess, at lunch, and immediately after school. I protested this directive because these trips definitely interfered with my school day, which I explained to him was why I was at Buckhorn. He was not moved by my argument.

One day soon after this directive, something happened at school, I cannot even remember what it was, that prevented me from getting to the chickens at recess. Mr. Brown saw me on campus and called me into his classroom at the end of the day. He pulled out a four-inch paddle and gave me several smacks. Of course, it hurt. My pride was hurt more. Never in my life had a teacher challenged my integrity, much less paddle me. When I later reported what had happened to me on one of my home visits, I had to plead with my father not to come to Buckhorn in my defense. My father may have felt that he could discipline his children as needed—even shoot at them if he was drunk; and he had even cautioned us if we got a paddling at school, we would get another when we got home. But in this case, his anger was not directed at me but at Mr. Brown.

Neither Mr. Brown nor I spoke again about the incident; but in my work, I learned something about chickens that has helped me understand human behavior. Individually, you can teach both chickens and human beings much. Collectively, however, much behavior from chickens and humans on an IQ test measures on a scale under the classification of "combined dumb." I also have observed that actions of chickens and humans can quickly resort to mob behavior. Even loud thunder can cause chickens to all bunch together which often results in death for some of them from suffocation. This same phenomenon has occurred when stores advertise some ridiculous price on an item for sale. And like chickens, humans often engage in pecking order socialization. If one is different enough to draw attention, others will quickly recognize this; and through being "pecked," the chicken or person learns its place in the social order. Among the chickens at Buckhorn, some poor souls even separated themselves at roosting time. I occasionally witnessed some of this same withdrawal behavior from some of the boys in my dormitory who were teased or bullied.

As if eating their eggs was not enough, another calamity struck the flock later the next year. I began noticing some hens with bloody diarrhea. With fear, I reported the problem to Mr. Brown. He said it looked like coccidiosius. To respond to the problem, Mr. Brown said all the saw dust bedding would have to be removed. He handed me a shovel and told me to begin. I emptied out the house, and fresh saw dust was installed. Even with this effort, the problem persisted. I have since learned that to really have solved this problem, medicinal treatment should have been added through food and water, and the new bedding needed to be clean and dry. During my time at Buckhorn, no antibiotics were provided. In addition, the new saw dust quickly drew dampness, which promoted the disease.

No more punishments were handed out to me. But our chicken flock was devastated. I am not sure if the school went out of the poultry business at the time, but I believe it did. In the meantime, I had let it out that I could also milk a cow, a very much in demand skill at Buckhorn. Within a few weeks, my job assignment was switched to the morning milk crew.

CHAPTER 8

McKenzie Meltdown

From the very early years of Witherspoon College, strong support was provided for people with health problems or for those who had personal difficulties in their lives. The Association built a hospital, which became one of school's most outstanding services; though the building sat idle when I first went to Buckhorn. Mr. Murdoch even went so far as to build a house for just two sisters with tuberculosis so they could continue their education. Special interest in the care of orphans was also a concern of Harvey and Louise Murdoch. Having none of their own, they adopted three children. Their interest was shared by benefactors of the Lafayette Avenue Church. Two of those members, Miss Charlotte Worthington and her sister, joined the group of earlier supporters of the school. They funded first a small building for orphans. Later the name of a magnificent building to house all the younger girls bore the name of Worthington Hall. The entrance to the building on one end had a wide staircase ascending seventeen steps from the roadway to a covered porch roof held up by stately columns. The structure itself was located higher on the mountain side and stood as a serene sentinel over the entire Witherspoon College campus.

My job as "chicken boy" took me by the building every time I did my work. On Valentine's Day in 1953 as I finished my work and headed back to my own dormitory, I looked up at the building and saw smoke billowing from the roof. At first, I had no concern because I felt someone had just stoked a fire to better heat the building. Then I noticed the smoke was not coming from the chimneys but from the roof itself.

At that point, I broke into a run down the road, up the stairs, and into the building where normally I would not have dared to enter. I called out to Sarah Collins, the housemother in charge of the care of the young girls. In my panicky voice, I informed Mrs. Collins that it looked to me as if the building was on fire. It was, and fortunately the notice was early enough for her to collect all the girls and evacuate with no one being lost or hurt. Very soon the billowing smoke gave way to leaping flames that quickly engulfed the entire building. The logs had seasoned for almost five decades which meant once a fire started there was no way it was going to be extinguished. To me, it appeared the fire started in upper levels, perhaps around a chimney, which also would have made it difficult to do anything to get it stopped. Only fate determined that no children died from smoke inhalation or from the flames themselves.

The location of the building and the flames from the fire quickly caught the attention of everybody in the community. Osha Keen, who kept a somewhat infrequent diary, recorded her observations of the event:

> "The Girls' Home burned today. A very few things saved. Mrs. Collin's piano was saved.
> "It was a beautiful building—in a beautiful place. The first you saw coming into Buckhorn. Somehow it stood out so serene—never alone—a pity indeed."

Having already experienced a devastating fire in the mid-forties that destroyed the dormitory for older boys, the flames of Worthington Hall were further warning to school authorities. In the meantime, those in charge relocated the girls to the original orphanage building just around the hill; and life continued as usual.

With this repeat of a devastating event, one would ask why no defenses were put in place to prevent more fires. A review of the minutes of the Buckhorn Association indicates the issue had not gone without being addressed. The minutes of a meeting of the Board of Managers of the Presbyterian Orphans Home Society for December 10, 1945, references a letter sent by the Secretary to the United Mutual Fire Insurance Company increasing the amount of insurance on certain pieces of the Home property. A committee was also established "to give further study to the insurance situation. " What became of the "study" is unknown. I found no further mention of this in any future minutes of the organization, so perhaps insurance could not be obtained for these one-of-a-kind structures or else the cost was too high to pay for the coverage. Or perhaps only limited coverage was obtained.

The Buckhorn Association was also aware of the age and the outdated infrastructure of the buildings and had begun a campaign to add facilities made of native rock to replace the log structures. Evidently the boys' dormitory was to be the architectural model for the entire campus. In the fall of the preceding year, the Association had tried to get the changes underway. A campaign was started to obtain funding for the dormitory for the older girls. The current dormitory was known as Englis Hall, after the middle name of Bertha Englis Sayre, for whom two buildings on the campus were named— the other being the Sayre Primary Building. The building fund was to total $100,000, with the goal being to collect $25,000 from Brooklyn friends, $25,000 from supporters in Hazard, $25,000 from the Synod of the Presbyterian Church of Kentucky, and $25,000 from direct solicitation of other friends.

This plan was too late. Just thirty-four days after the loss of Worthington Hall, on March 19, 1953, a calamity of even greater damage occurred. This time Englis Hall, McKenzie Hall which housed the dining hall and food preparation facilities, and Faith Hall which originally served as the domestic science program all met their doom by a huge fire. The fire started in the Englis Hall dormitory but quickly spread to the two other buildings because of their close proximity. I recall the fire was so powerful that weeks later after the buildings stood no more, the smoldering embers made it still too hot for me to walk over the area. This time I saw nothing of the early start of the fire. My first vision was of flames coming from the upper windows and from the roofs.

Fortunately, fate intervened and once more no lives were lost in the fire.

Again, Osha Keen recorded her feelings in her diary:

> "The Girls Dormitory, Dining Hall, and old Home Ec building burned today—a pitiful sight—one that was hard to see.
> "Remembering all the years they had been in use. . . . The principle of their existence. . . . No wonder someone said it was major loss."

Mrs. Keen's statements were an understatement. Aside from the scare everyone experienced, the immediate question was how the school could even continue, as these buildings were an integral part of the operation. Englis Hall was a three-story structure first erected in 1905 and renovated three times to modernize the infrastructure and to increase the number of girls who could be accommodated there. In all, there were twelve dormitory rooms. Originally, each room contained two double beds, but like other dormitory rooms at the school, surplus World War II bunk beds replaced the double beds.

This time, Dr. Gabbard and his staff met the challenge of lost housing by re-opening the unused hospital and converting it to dormitory use.

McKenzie Hall, the Refectory, the gift from the architect of the original Times Square Building in New York, served not only as the dining hall, but in many ways was the center of life for those who lived on campus. It was here girls were taught how to cook and properly serve food. Often faculty members who lived on campus dispersed themselves to individual tables and taught students proper table manners and etiquette. When students first entered the facility, they waited until a second bell rang and then proceeded to take their places at the dining tables. Everyone remained seated until the food was served and until everyone finished the meal. I laughed when I once read a criticism of the Soul Winners for believing they could save people's souls by teaching them which side of the plate a fork should be placed. The criticism should surely be rejected in regard to soul saving, but unquestionably etiquette was an instructional goal for those of us who attended Buckhorn.

This agenda had to be changed after the fire when food services were moved across the campus to a building that looks as if it may also have been military surplus. Now everything operated cafeteria style, except for some hold-over perceptions of Mrs. Alta Wooton, the head of food services. Mrs. Wooton had her own beliefs as to how students should come and go and what their behavioral expectancies should be while they ate. In this regard, she was definitely "old school." I believe she made up dining hall rules as she saw fit on any given day. If she changed a rule, you generally found out about it when you unknowingly broke the rule. With little explanation as to what a hungry person had done wrong, a violation of Mrs. Wooton's rules could easily end up with the miscreant being summarily dismissed from the dining hall—resulting in indigestion from what the waif had been able to consume and at the same time an empty pit in his stomach that lasted until he might be allowed to eat again.

The third building lost in this fire, Faith Hall, was built in the 20's and in many ways served as a "finishing school" for girls. It was the domestic science building, where nutrition, sewing, fashion design, weaving, hygiene, and home nursing all were taught. In the early years, style shows were annual highlights in the program. By the 50's, home economics had moved to Lafayette Hall, the main school building. For a time, the building served as housing for instructors. I believe it was empty when it burned.

These two fires in quick succession created a lot of talk around the campus. I heard that arson may have been involved, with the fires set by a disturbed and angry student. But I never learned the outcome of any investigation, nor in my review of the financial records have I found any significant receipts of any insurance to cover the loss.

Whatever the cause, the loss of the buildings was horrendous. Nevertheless, life went on for all of us. Those of us who lived in the boys' dormitory experienced little change in our routines and also had little appreciation for even the atmosphere of living in the log dormitories in the first place. Our building— other than being an echo chamber and having smelly and terrible tasting water—was modern in comparison to the other dormitories. The girls, however, lost all their personal belongings right down to the mattresses on which they slept. They had to adjust to these losses at the same time they had to deal with their cramped new quarters in buildings that were not meant to serve as dormitory space. The lives of most girls in the dormitories, however, had already been filled with loss, abandonment, and poverty. The fires were just one more bit of bad fate they had to endure. And endure they did. They moved to new quarters, put on more second-hand dresses, started a new collection of meaningful personal items, and went on as best they could with their school activities.

We as students focused on the work and school life because that was all we knew. Behind the scenes, however, the school was financially devastated. Contacts were made with any organization that might come to the rescue. Since the death of Mr. Underwood about fifteen years before these fires, it was clear no one single donor was going to surface in Brooklyn. The fortunes of many of the early benefactors there had changed after the great Depression. Dr. Gabbard did not have the same personal connections with people in Brooklyn as had Dr. Murdoch. And as early supporters grew old, they were not replaced by a younger generation of people with the resources and interest in a place as remote from them as Buckhorn, Kentucky.

This meant help if it were coming at all would have to come from somewhere else. Fortunately, help did come from a somewhat unlikely source—from the E. O. Robinson Mountain Fund. The fund made an immediate gift toward rebuilding, and a conference and study was held to suggest the possibility of an outright merger of the Robinson Foundation and the Buckhorn Association.

Though it was almost a certainty that no student at Buckhorn had ever heard of E.O. Robinson or his partner Fredrick W. Mobray of the Mobray-Robinson Lumber Company based in Cincinnati, Ohio, these two individuals have a history almost as old as Harvey Murdoch. In 1908, the two purchased nearly 15,000 acres of land in the counties of Perry, Knott, and Breathitt. They might have been viewed by some as "robber barons" because they made a fortune by taking virgin timber from the land.

However, Mr. Robinson, if he were a robber baron, certainly

redeemed himself. He and Mr. Mobray in 1924 donated their acreage to the University of Kentucky, where the school has established an agricultural research center. One of the first activities of this program was to remove the American chestnut trees that had been killed by a blight caused by a parasite introduced by nursery stock from Asia. Before the blight, these magnificent trees grew straight and tall without branches for as high as fifty feet. The trees, in addition, to the nuts, were a lumber source for telegraph poles, railroad ties, and roofing shingles. By the time, I got to Buckhorn, the only thing I knew about the chestnut tree was that it was a dead wood that my granny and I often tried to find for firewood. It was seasoned, easy to kindle a fire with, light to carry, and easy to cut.

In addition to the Foundation, Mr. Robinson also established a Fund, which today is administered by the Board of Trustees of the University of Kentucky. In 1991, a plan was put in motion to set aside coal and timber royalties from a 5,000-acre section of the Robinson Forest to support economic and community efforts in Appalachian Kentucky. Annual full-ride college scholarships are awarded to students from twenty-nine Eastern Kentucky counties.

In 1953, however, it appears the "Fund" was money still looking for a home or for a use that might fulfill the mission of the program envisioned by Mr. Robinson. In November, 1953, at the meeting of the Buckhorn Association in the home of Mrs. C. Vanderbilt Barton in Brooklyn, Dr. Gabbard noted that 347 students were enrolled at Buckhorn at the beginning of the school year. He further informed the members that temporary arrangements for dormitory accommodations and dining facilities had been completed. And an organization and plan had been perfected to raise $320,000 to provide for new buildings. A total of $135,000 had already been guaranteed. The proposal to consolidate the Buckhorn Association with the E.O. Robinson Mountain Fund was also presented to the members.

On December 7, 1953, an agreement was reached for the Buckhorn Association to transfer its real estate and all other assets—except the church property—to the E. O. Robinson Mountain Fund. In return, the E.O. Robinson Fund agreed to continue to carry on the work established by the Buckhorn Association, Inc., for the education and betterment of the children of the Mountain Area of Eastern Kentucky.

The merger was finalized in April, 1954. Dr. Gabbard reported to the Buckhorn Association members that a fire-proof building to replace Worthington Home had been completed. The new building was built to hold forty children and had dining room facilities for twenty additional children from the little boys' home.

The budget for the school program was to be underwritten from the Robinson Fund and to be supplemented by additional gifts from other sources.

The first responsibility now from the Buckhorn Association itself was to provide for the maintenance of the church and its ministry. A minimum budget for that purpose was set at $6,000. An additional $6,000 was to be sought for the improvement of the church and the manse.

The total assets of the Buckhorn Association turned over to the Robinson Mountain Fund on June 30, 1954, totaled almost $404,000. These assets included all property except for the church and the manse. For that program, the budget for the Buckhorn Association itself was reduced to $4,400.

At the time of the transfer of property, the care of ten wards of the Presbyterian Synod Home for Children was also assigned to the Robinson Fund. These wards included two families of five children each. Of one group I have personal memory. One morning Dr. Gabbard came out of his house to find five children standing in front of his house with all their personal belongings in brown paper bags. Their parents had left them there and disappeared. The youngest was just a toddler. I personally recall the oldest boy. He and I were on work assignments together on many occasions. Evidently, he felt I was the one person on campus from whom who he could win a fight; for he started one with me almost every time we were not supervised. In actuality, I never won any of those fights; but he did not win either. The fights generally recessed when one or the other of us knocked the other off the fence around the barn, only to be continued the next day or so. To this day, I have no idea what any of the conflict was all about. Officially, this agreement between the Robinson Fund and the Buckhorn Association identified to me people actually labeled as orphans. At the time I gave it no further thought. Though the children never went home, their daily lives seemed about the same as the rest of us.

In November, 1954, the Association expressed deep regret on the passing of Mrs. Edward F. Geer, who in her will left a provision for a bequest of $10,000 to the Association. Since the responsibility for the Association was now only to the church, it was an irony that the building designed and financed by the Geers would now be the beneficiary of the last thing she did on earth.

By this time, the annual budget for the school and orphanage amounted to $60,000, of which $40,000 was provided by the Robinson Fund. The $20,000 remainder was to come from local support, the Synod of Kentucky, and other friends of the institution. The Synod was not an easy mark for its part. Dr. Gabbard wrote a collection letter in April, 1955, indicating that a check for $1,249.80 had been received for the months of October, November, and December. But Dr. Gabbard's letter was a request for the Synod's remittance for the months of January, February, and March.

The Robinson Fund soon found that it did not want to be in the orphanage business. So in May, 1956, just two years after it had taken responsibility for Buckhorn, the Fund entered into an agreement with the Presbyterian Synod Home for Children that gave the responsibility for the proper care and maintenance of children of the mountain area of Eastern Kentucky back to the Presbyterian Church. In doing so, the Fund agreed to turn over all the Buckhorn assets previously assigned to it. The Mountain Fund further agreed to contribute $40,000 per year for at least five years to support the transferred program.

Earlier in September, 1955, a letter from The Board of Pensions of the Presbyterian Church in the United States of America regarding the transfer of assets questioned whether the transfer should be done immediately or over a period of time. The letter also referenced the end of service of Dr. Gabbard to the school—at least in an administrative capacity. Dr. Gabbard had agreed to a proposal that he take up promotional work and be relieved of all administrative duties. Later in my life when I learned of this agreement and knowing that Dr. Gabbard had graduated from Berea College, I was reminded of my great-uncle's assessment of the success of Berea graduates for being professional beggars. Here to me was living proof of Uncle Herbert's assertions.

By this time, it was also likely that Dr. Gabbard felt he had done all he could to carry on with the mission he inherited from Harvey Murdoch. Events had certainly been trying for the twenty years he had been at the helm of the school, and Dr. Gabbard has been called a saint for all of his efforts. There is no question that he was a tireless worker to benefit the school and those students who came to Witherspoon. On the other hand, some of his trials, in my opinion, were due to his own character. When I compare Mr. Murdoch and Dr. Gabbard, the latter did not appear to have the same single-mindedness of purpose as did Mr. Murdoch; and perhaps he became distracted by other goals he had in life, such as running for political office. My opinion should not be interpreted to demean him or to diminish the contributions Dr. Gabbard made to the lives of many of us who could not have received our educations without Buckhorn.

Shortly after the transfer of assets back from the Robinson Fund, the Synod of Kentucky established the Presbyterian Child Welfare Agency, which though changed in operation and control to this day continues at least a part of the mission promulgated by the Society of Soul Winners. Association history reveals the Agency began a program of ministry to homeless children planned in accordance with the best advice and direction available. Merged with the Buckhorn funds in support of this organization were the funds of the Grundy Farm and Home and the Presbyterian Synod's Home for Children, giving a total in invested endowment of almost $600,000. In addition to these funds, the Robinson Fund continued to contribute $40,000 annually for another five years.

After the "retirement" of Dr. Gabbard, the new program obtained the services of Reverend Robert G. McClure as the Director of Administration at Buckhorn. The person who first brought me to Buckhorn was coming there himself—just as I was leaving. It was noted that someone else would be sought to be the pastor of the Buckhorn church, a good idea in my opinion, considering many of Reverend McClure's sermons I personally endured. In addition, a trained social worker was to be added to the staff to make needed studies and investigations necessary for the understanding and development of the children. In retrospect, I am glad I was not at Buckhorn for such study and investigation.

Dr. and Mrs. Gabbard left shortly and moved to Berea where the office of Director of Promotion was established. The

Office did not exist for very long. The minutes of the Buckhorn Association of 1960 reflected a moment of silent prayer in tribute to Dr. Gabbard and other members whose names were read as having passed on that year.

One of those whose name was read was Edith Underwood Conard, who had served as Secretary of the Buckhorn Association. In her last minutes, she recorded the Association had agreed to negotiate the transfer of church property to the Ebenezer Presbytery. In proposing this transfer, it was moved and seconded that the Presbyterian Welfare Agency should ask the Synod of Kentucky to return sufficient land (about 25 acres), part of it near the church for recreational purposes and part of it arable land for "God's Acres Program" for the benefit of the Buckhorn Church. To support for this goal, it was pointed out that Mr. Underwood and others bought and gave the land for the benefit of the church as well as the children, and the future needs of the church should be kept in mind.

Evidently, the Association felt that this transfer could be used for something profitable to help sustain the church. This last effort by the Buckhorn Association was not successful. This action also pretty much ended the relationship of Witherspoon College and the Lafayette Street Presbyterian Church in Brooklyn.

CHAPTER 9

Bovine Bitterness and Union Organizing

While efforts were being made to save Buckhorn from financial oblivion, most students simply went about daily business without much change. Personally, I actually began my second year at Buckhorn with a new found sense of freedom. I learned that if I walked to the top of the hill above the school, I could hitch a ride with one of the coal trucks that ran from there all the way to a tipple at Proctor, across the Kentucky River at Beattyville. From there, I could hitch another ride for about five miles to St. Helens. If I got that far, I could walk the rest of the way up Dunigan's Branch Road and over the Long Shoal Hill, still a good two miles.

Returning to Buckhorn, however, was more complicated. The coal trucks did not run on Sundays, which meant another way had to be found. My father discovered the L & N Rail Road still ran a passenger train daily from Lexington to Hazard. The train did not stop at St. Helens any more, but it could be flagged down if the rider stood across the tracks from the station building. (I learned this the hard way. Once, I tried flagging the train from the station side; and the train blew right by me.) Passenger traffic at this point was absolutely the lowest priority for the rail road company, so the printed schedule was not worth the paper on which it was printed. One could be sure the train would not be early. But it was anyone's guess just how late it would be. The timing was critical for me. I had to ride the train to Chavies and be there in time to catch the last bus that stopped there on its route from Hazard to Buckhorn. If the train missed the connection, I was again in a position to try to hitch the ten-mile trip on to Buckhorn. On one occasion, darkness was falling when the train finally arrived. I was on the verge of panic as to how I would finish the trip after dark. To my rescue came the father of classmate David Pennington who quickly recognized my predicament. Out of the kindness of a stranger, he invited me to stay the night, fed me supper and breakfast, and packed me on the school bus the next morning.

My trips home were rare, but just knowing they were possible gave me a sense of independence. Even infrequent riders on the train by this time were quite unusual, so much so the conductor eventually struck up a little conversation with me. He was totally unaware, however, that on one trip I carried a water snake in a half-gallon jar to take back to show to my biology teacher. I had mistaken the snake's head for a chub minnow and had caught it with my bare hands. My teacher informed that that I had been lucky. The snake, he said, was not venomous but was one of the most aggressive snakes in the area.

The memorable teacher for me that year was Mr. Cheek, a graduate of Centre College. Mr. Cheek was a gentle soul but totally unprepared for the urchins he faced in his English class. Each day he sat behind his desk, with his spectacles drooped low over his nose, and read aloud in a monotone voice literature from *Adventures in Appreciation*. His volume was so low he could not be heard past the front row even if a student wanted to follow along. That was no worry, for no one wanted to hear him read. Left on their own, many of the students invented their own mischief. The class was very much motivated by adventure but had little to offer in the way of appreciation of literature. On one occasion, the action got out of hand; and someone broke a window. Finally, that noise was so loud it actually caught Mr. Cheek's attention. He reported the incident to the principal but had no clue as to what had happened or who had done the damage. Of course, when questioned, no one in class could understand what had happened either.

Mr. Cheek's tests were about as instructional as his teaching. On one test, I recall he actually asked the following question: "What was the color of the dog's eyes on page 57?" There was no way most of the students were going to pass his tests. However, because I liked to read, I was generally familiar with the stories. Armed with this information, I made decent grades. Others soon learned this and asked for my help, which I reckoned would not be so wrong considering my opinion as to the unfairness of the tests in the first place. Unfortunately, Mr. Cheek, who did not know who broke a window in his class, had enough detective skills to catch me cheating. He handled the case by saying, "Alex, I would never have believed this of you." I had very little recourse but to admit my sin. He took no further action, thinking shame would be the appropriate consequence.

Mr. Cheek had other idiosyncrasies. He drove a new Pontiac car and on one occasion took a group of us somewhere. Being low on gas, he stopped and added some fuel to his tank. He then wrote a check for fifty cents to pay for his purchase. Other students have told me they once hot-wired his car and drove it right by him without him noticing at all.

Mr. Cheek's career at Buckhorn was not a long one. But it was not my last encounter with him. When I enrolled in a zoology class in college, I walked in to my first session and found no other than Mr. Cheek as my teacher. I recall that on one occasion the class went on a bird-watching field hike. Mr. Cheek had the only pair of field glasses. Frequently, he would become excited and point out some bird across the mountain from the one on which we stood. "Do you all see the Kentucky Warbler on that oak tree limb?" he asked. From where we stood, we could only see the other mountain, no individual tree, and certainly no bird. Being older, students now had become more skilled in the art of sarcasm. In response to his question, one of the more creative students, responded with, "Yes, I see it; and how about the Mother Kildeer in her nest on the ground just to the right of the tree?" Mr. Cheek was dumb-founded. He adjusted his glasses and peered for several minutes before admitting he simply had not seen what the student professed to see. The student had the nerve to ask for extra credit for his keen observation.

Tests were no different in zoology than they had been in English class. For our final examination, Mr. Cheek held up pictures on 3 X 5 cards of various birds he felt we should recognize while at the same time he played a recording of the bird call. Our job was to identify the bird. Those of us seated on the front row could see the bird; those in the back saw just a little bit of color on a card. But fate came to our rescue. Each of the bird cards had the name of the bird printed below the picture. In holding up the card while at the same time trying to control the needle arm on the record player, Mr. Cheek's hand invariably slipped and exposed the print below the picture. I guess I still had not learned any moral lesson from Mr. Cheek. I wrote down the name of the bird while simultaneously whispering it aloud as I wrote. One could hear a chain of whispers moving through the room as each card was shown.

As for my work experience, I had already received my first corporal punishment for my failure with chickens. My firm belief to this day is that I received unjust punishment. But I later got some revenge against Mr. Brown for using the paddle on me. This time I could have had no complaints had he done so again.

That year, the farm had produced an abundant crop of potatoes. They had been stored for keeping in the basement of the log cathedral when someone finally noticed that some of the potatoes were rotting. Mr. Brown assigned a few of us to sort out the good ones from the bad ones. In our boredom with the work, one boy threw a rotten potato at another on the work committee. Immediately war was declared. The pillars holding up the church made good fortresses. We soon built up dumps of ammunition of rotten potatoes; and our missiles flew through the basement, sometimes hitting their mark of another worker but mostly just making a splat. The sounds and smells grew with each projectile launched. While we were in full battle, we noticed a figure framed in the doorway. We assumed it was an enemy trying to escape. That was not allowed under our declared war-time convention. Both sides of the war then declared war on the person in the doorway. Eventually, we all found out that the person was not a worker but was Mr. Brown himself who had come to see how we were doing. Our direct hits on Mr. Brown bordered on overkill before we recognized what we had done.

For some reason, Mr. Brown did not punish me or anybody else, perhaps because he was too embarrassed to let it out that the potatoes had been inappropriately stored under the church in the first place. There was a repercussion, however. The stench was so bad that church services had to be moved from the church to the cafeteria for the next two weeks.

Mr. Brown was actually a very popular teacher on campus. He was socially active and evidently quite skilled in square dancing. He and I somehow declared a truce, for I made good grades in his class. With his backing and that of several other students in the class I was nominated and won the election for District Secretary of the Future Farmers of America. I think most of the honor came from my skill in the use of Robert's Rules of Order and from the sympathy of my fellow classmates. They worked harder for my election than I did. The thing I remember most about it was that I also was the recipient for free of a coveted FFA jacket, one I could never have afforded otherwise.

It was later that year that I revealed I knew how to milk a cow. When Mr. Johnson passed this information on to Mr. Brown, I was immediately assigned to the morning milk crew. I thought of the assignment as a promotion, but I soon learned it was a job no one wanted. The crew consisted of four boys who got up each morning at 4:30 A.M. and pushed a wheel barrow for about two miles to the barn. The wheelbarrow had been rigged to hold two ten-gallon milk cans. Our duties called for each of us to milk four cows and return to campus by 6:15 A.M.

In performing these duties, I learned that the school had two farms: one located down the river where the barn and silo were located, and the other, the Anderson farm, some distance away. It was this farm consisting of about 300 acres that had been purchased much later than the big farm paid for by Mr. Underwood, even when the New York benefactors had been reluctant to provide the financing for the additional acreage.

In addition to its valuable timber, the Anderson farm was used to pasture cows until they had calves and were "fresh," that is ready to be milked. The cows were then transported to the big farm. For most of the animals, this was their first experience at being handled by human beings. The uncivilized heifers did not take too kindly to being handled by young boys who in turn had little interest in animal husbandry.

The standing rule from Mrs. Alta Wooton, our food services director, was that everyone had to be ready to eat at the last bell which rang at 6:30 A. M. She was not amenable to any exceptions. No matter what happened in our work at the barn, if we did not get the milk back to the kitchen and then ourselves to the dormitory to wash and change our clothes by the second bell, we were refused breakfast. Mrs. Wooton felt the punishment would modify our behavior. What she did not fully understand, however, was that missing some of the productions of the domestic science program she oversaw were not always punishment. Burnt gravy or biscuits hard enough for use in a baseball game was hardly motivation for us to play a game of beat the clock. Long term, her adherence to the rules still has not made me all that eager to rush to the breakfast table.

Getting back on time was important to us though, with breakfast being just one reason. Yet every day began with an inherent problem. One of our crew was a heavy sleeper. Because he was the oldest, it was his responsibility to wake the rest of the crew. Holding Rip Van Winkle responsible for this assignment was a waste. He never heard the clock, and he never woke anyone. I, on the other hand, woke up from my own internal clock and voluntarily took on the job. There was one complication. Not only did our crew chief not wake easily; when he finally did, he was literally fighting mad. I avoided being clobbered by keeping my distance, poking him with a broom, and fleeing to the barn with the speed of Jesse Owens. Sometime later, the boy dragged himself to the barn. He never mentioned my hitting him with the stick, but he often complained that I had not awakened him.

In addition to the inconvenience of having to get up so early, the morning milk crew operated with several other disadvantages. For one thing, we began our duties in the dark almost all the time. When the weather turned cold, we really suffered. Most of us did not have many clothes anyway, and we never had enough to protect us from the bitter winds and piercing rain and snow as we made the daily voyage to the barn. Sometimes we wrapped towels around our heads and necks. When the towels got wet, they froze on our heads. To the cows, we looked like nomads just pulled out of cold storage. Just our showing up often scared the poor beasts.

Under these conditions, few of us arrived at our jobs with a real positive attitude. We were in no mood to tolerate any bad behavior from the cows, but we often got it. Cows, when upset, can be very stubborn. Frequently, they objected to even moving into the stanchions to get them into a position for milking. Their attitudes did not improve when we tried to clean them for milking, and neither did ours if they did not cooperate. They often responded by kicking at us and at the buckets we tried to get under them. Cows often are referred to in Biblical terms as "dumb animals." Rest assured, they only got that name because they have limited language, not because of low cognitive ability. They have a great sense of timing and an even better awareness of where they are in space. While they nonchalantly concentrate on eating, cows can kick a bucket right out of a person's hands without even looking. They also have other weapons at their disposal. When disturbed, they can manufacture freshly made cow pies which they can aim with deadly accuracy at a bucket a person might be holding. If on occasion, their swings are a ball and not a strike, their fallback maneuver is to swing their tails loaded with the fresh manure and hit the person holding the bucket. The result can be a near concussion and a head so slimy no health professional will touch it.

With these inherited skills and their total immodesty, it was not uncommon for some of our cows to literally kick the bucket and spill the milk just at the point when the milking was almost completed. At first, if the milk was contaminated with cow dung, the milk crew threw out the milk. Mrs. Wooton, however, was well aware of how much milk our cans should have. She always insisted on getting a full load. Our stories told with one hundred percent honesty did not move her one bit. She told us she had heard too many lies from milk crews to ever be fooled again.

Our legal arguments failed us and left the crew to find a new tactic for future incidents. If the milk was spilled or polluted, we covered ourselves by filling the cans with water to make it look like the same amount that was expected from us. But this approach did not work either. As the milk clabbered, Mrs. Wooton's keen eyesight picked up there was far too much whey. She responded as customary by refusing us breakfast. Known by this time for my quick retorts, I once asked her why she bothered to cook at all since she never seemed to want anybody to eat. For this remark, she doubled my punishment to no breakfast for the next two days, which was a real incentive for me to get the milk back on time the next day.

Finally, not being the most creative group ever assigned to a milk crew, we could think of nothing else to do. From then on, if a cow stepped in the bucket or used the bucket as her personal toilet, we still just dumped everything into the milk can. On receipt of the product, the girls who worked in the kitchen did what they always did. They strained the milk through cheese cloth and served it up nice and cold to the unsuspecting hungry mouths that passed through the food line. I swear the milk sometimes had a light shade of green to it when the kitchen girls poured it into glasses. Soon most of the students caught on that if the milk crew drank the milk, things had gone well at the barn. But if we pushed our glasses back, the tables all had full tumblers when everyone finished the meal. Mrs. Wooton tried to put in a new rule about finishing everything on your plate, but even she had no success in enforcing this one.

Later, as I was leaving Buckhorn for college, Reverend McClure took me to look over the campus of Pikeville as he had done earlier for me to look at Buckhorn. He evidently knew something I did not—that he would soon be in charge of the school program. This time, the preacher did not mention John Witherspoon. He was more interested in giving me his assessment of the status of Buckhorn. In doing so, he specifically pointed out that he thought there were some unsanitary conditions in the kitchen. He was concerned the food might make children sick, especially having them drink unpasteurized milk. He spoke aloud his thinking to me that he was inclined to do away with some of the farming activities and that he felt students should be provided milk in paper cartons. I just listened silently and agreed with him. At the same time, I did voice that the milking program provided eight boys with work opportunities to help them pay their way through school.

Being so intimate with the cows assigned to us, some I remember better than many of the students. Since the cows came to us with practically no prior human contact, they had no given names. The milk crew got the privilege of naming them. Previous reports have been that out of respect for their largess, many of the cows were named after New York benefactors. Early cows at the farm were prized stock used in establishing a good blood line for farmers in the area. Naming a cow after a benefactor would have been seen as an honor, not an insult. That tradition certainly changed with the milk crews of my time. Cows that were hard to train or those who refused to cooperate with us were instead named after the ugliest girls on campus. We made sure the girls knew this. This knowledge likely explains the care the girls took in straining the milk. It also was a likely reason why I had such a hard time getting a date for the junior-senior prom.

Many of the cows were treated cruelly. Some of them lost their spirit and gave in to whatever mean thing some of the boys did to them. One we named Pig—the same nickname of a girl with wide nostrils—became the grand dam of the herd and stood quietly while the boys did anything they wanted to do to her—as long as she was eating. One day a member of the crew in a mood more foul than usual, stuck a hose up Pig's butt and turned on the water. Pig never flinched as the cold water swelled her four stomach chambers to capacity and more. At that moment, she shot a hydrant of green water all over the boy. That was the last time he gave a cow an enema.

My favorite bovine friend was Star, who escaped the negative smear of being named after an ugly girl. Star was added to the herd because she was a Holstein and produced two full buckets of milk at each milking. Though much lower in butterfat than milk from the prized herd of Jerseys for which the school was famous, Star's production certainly expanded the number of glasses that could be filled by the milk crew's efforts. Socially, however, Star's presence seemed to be a sacrilege to the rest of the herd. She was huge and not compact like the others. She was a social isolate. The other boys did not want to milk her because she gave two or three times more milk than the other cows. Star and I built camaraderie with each other. She literally followed me to the milk parlor when I arrived at the barn each morning. I could always tell from her eyes if the evening crew had been mean to her the night before. In such cases if there was time, I spent a few minutes scratching the white spot on her head which had resulted in her name.

The fires and resulting generous gift by the Robinson Fund actually produced one improvement noticed by everyone who worked on the farm. We did not know where it came from, but we were very surprised when Dr. Gabbard purchased a new, army green International pick-up truck for farm use, indicating some priority for the farm versus the displaced girls. Riding in the truck became the highest honor for the boys. Mr. Brown and our dormitory director Mr. Johnson took turns hauling students to and from their various chores. Riding up front indicated a position of prestige and could lead to out right fist fights if the social pecking order was threatened. Even riding in the back of the truck, however, caused such excitement that made it difficult to meditate and pray if you were caught on the road when the 6:00 P.M. prayer bell echoed through the countryside.

Actually, Mr. Brown and Mr. Johnson only transported the boys whose work hours were convenient for Mr. Brown and Mr. Johnson. The hours of the morning milk crew certainly did not qualify. While the evening crew rode to the barn and no longer had to push the wheelbarrow, the morning crew continued its usual routine. The evening crew rode; the morning crew walked and pushed.

As might be expected, the four of us complained. I was nominated by the group to do the talking. I used my best FFA speaking skills, but nothing changed. The evening crew even taunted us about our misfortune. We thought we had found a way out of our circumstances one day when major flood waters rose almost to the roadway of the old WPA bridge we had to cross to get to the barn. I suggested to the others that we ought to push the wheelbarrow into the rushing torrent of water and then question what the evening crew had done with it. My calculation was that we could get a little revenge with them by blaming them for the loss since they certainly were the last to have seen the wheelbarrow. Further, if things worked out, perhaps we would also be riding to and from the barn. Also, with the swift current, it seemed likely the wheelbarrow would end up forty miles downstream never to be seen again, which would cover our criminal actions. Clearly, on this occasion, my sinful plotting was evidence that I had dropped below the morality bar Coach Johnson had urged us to set for ourselves. I rationalized my behavior by feeling it was justification for unfair treatment.

The plan did work for a few days. However, when the flood waters receded, just below the bridge almost exactly where we unceremoniously dumped it, the wheel barrow stood out in clear view of anyone who looked over the bridge side. Evidently it caught on the rocks and withstood a natural catastrophe that would easily have washed a house down the river. Word spread quickly of its whereabouts, probably from some afternoon snitch.

Those of us on the morning crew were incredulous as to how the vehicle got there. But any protestations from us would have made no difference anyway. Mr. Brown announced to us that from now on, the crew would have to carry the cans to and from the barn. Each can was as tall as our waists and when filled with milk weighed about a hundred pounds. Making the trip back to campus on foot with this amount of weight was quite a chore, but we got no relief. Mrs. Wooton did not vary her requirement that we get the milk back to her on time. In fact, our actions apparently verified her judgment that we were all totally worthless.

In my one attempt as a union activist, I decided to appeal Mr. Brown's decision directly to Dr. Gabbard. Somehow, I summoned the courage to knock on his door and tell him of the injustice. Dr. Gabbard was known for his inviting personality to wealthy donors and voters, but he was not seen as very approachable by most students. In fact, the only good thing I personally could say about Dr. Gabbard myself is that he once ran for a political office as a Republican. In his first run, he actually did quite well. He lost by only about 500 votes in a heavy Democratic district. But he was clobbered in the 1944 election, which was a year of a presidential vote. The ultimate success of his efforts as a candidate for U. S. Representative from Kentucky in the 7th District in 1942 and again in 1944 is that he has an alphabetical listing in *The Political Graveyard*, where it is also noted that he served as an alternate delegate to the National Republican Conventions in 1944 and 1948. Dr. Gabbard and his wife Myrtle, who in the eyes of many people who knew them intimately was the power behind the throne, frequently were seen traveling in their Cadillac automobile while occupying their home on campus. But they were also away from the school for long periods. In such times, they apparently were in residence in another home they owned in Owsley County.

The time their presence was felt most was when Dr. Gabbard gave one of his resounding sermons at the Log Cathedral. He spoke with the same volume and presence most of us imagine God used when He handed down The Ten Commandments to Moses. I remember none of the content of any of his sermons. But I do remember an incident somewhat comparable to the story of Dorothy Kelly who dropped her pencil during one of Harvey Murdoch's sermons. In this case, Tubby Boggs brought a marble to church and accidentally dropped it on the floor while Dr. Gabbard was making what I assume was a significant point in his sermon. An eerie silence descended on the church as the marble as from some kind of force of perpetual motion rolled and rolled on the floor. My own mind was filled with the words of the song "Nearer My God to Thee" as Dr. Gabbard stopped his sermon, came down from the pulpit, and stared poor Tubby directly in the eye. With a voice that could be heard through the immense space of the log cathedral, Dr.

Gabbard delivered a personal sermon to the young child with the whole congregation there to bear witness. I am confident that Tubby's personality was shaped permanently from that sermon. I heard he never played marbles again but sometime later in life took up mumbly peg, an exciting game played with a pocket knife.

Even with this experience as to Dr. Gabbard's power, the incident of the wheelbarrow so infuriated me that I was ready to confront whatever would be my fate. I marched myself over to his house and told him of the differences that were being made between the morning and evening crews. I also pointed out how unjust and inhumane it was for us to have to carry the milk back.

Dr. Gabbard responded to me with the same look on his face I recalled from the marble incident. After a long pause, he spoke. "Young man," he said, "I was a student at Buckhorn myself when things were a lot harder than they are now. You boys are very lucky to have people care for you the way we do here. You should be ashamed of yourself for bringing me this problem." After his brief statement, he turned, entered his home, and closed the door. I pondered on his response and thought perhaps I was not as grateful as I should be. At the same time, I also felt some progress with regard to getting the milk back to campus should have been made in the last forty years since Dr. Gabbard had been a student.

I retreated to my dorm room crestfallen and depressed. The rest of the crew wanted to know what happened and whether I was still in school. I said I doubted it. But since nothing happened further that day, I joined the group again the next morning to complete our chores. The more we struggled to get the cans back to campus, the angrier I became. Instead of taking the cans directly to the cafeteria to be greeted by Mrs. Wooton's happy face, I by myself instead dragged one of them over to Dr. Gabbard's porch and knocked on his door. At six-thirty in the morning, Dr. Gabbard was a little blurry-eyed when he opened the door; and his voice was even crustier than usual.

I figured I had nothing further to lose, so before he could deliver another sermon to me or immediately send me packing, I looked him straight in the eye and blurted out, "Dr. Gabbard, here is your milk."

"Why in the world did you bring it here instead of taking it to the kitchen where it belongs?" he boomed.

"This is just to show you that anything you did when you were in school, we can still do!" I said. And then with finality, I added, "But that still doesn't make it right!"

With that, I turned on my heels, went to my dormitory room, and started packing my bags. Now I was sure that I would be expelled. I did not bother with breakfast, but I did go to class.

For reasons I do not understand, no one said a word to me. Somehow the can of milk got to the cafeteria that day. By next morning, the crew discovered the wheelbarrow had been repaired. Members of the morning crew were still stuck with our same old routine. But the evening crew never teased us again. And for the most part, Mrs. Wooton at least for a time let up on us if we encountered a problem at the barn. That incident led me to conclude that Dr. Gabbard really did have a heart, even though to most of us he "hid that talent under a bushel."

Chapter 10

Oh, Henry!

A common trait of adolescence is rebellion. Human growth and development teaches us this phenomenon is due to brain development, which appears to show growth spurts in five discreet stages. One of the more pronounced stages occurs right before puberty, and not much else happens brain-wise during puberty itself. This likely explains why many authorities refer to adolescence as a "disease." The pre-adolescent brain growth stage for the first time enables youths to want to sort out right from wrong on their own rather than just accept or resist expectations of parents and teachers. My own myopic view of fairness was evidently a manifestation of this principle during some of my Buckhorn years.

In addition to either my previously recounted stupidity or courage for confronting the head of the school himself about the conditions faced by the morning milk crew, I also took some of this same attitude to class with me. One year, for instance, our chemistry teacher Mr. Eversole, who was also our principal, announced that all students who were eighteen years old with a 95% average would be excused from the final examination. I did the math. We only had one person in the class who met the age criterion, and who just by coincidence also had a 95% average. My own average happened to be 97%.

For certain, I complained about this arbitrary rule. I pointed out that my grades were higher than the beautiful brunette the teacher was rewarding, implying there might be some sinful reason for the rule he had forced on the class. Mr. Eversole got my point and responded with, "Alex, you have zero social skills." He then offered me vocational guidance right on the spot.

"I think you might best succeed in life by becoming a hermit," he told me.

I later shared this chemistry story with a good friend of mine from the class, Nella Johnson. She reminded me that she also had not taken the chemistry examination. I had never heard this and asked her why, while at the same time I pointed out to her that she did not meet the age criterion nor was she a brunette. Nella told me she had made a habit of skipping chemistry class. When caught and asked why by Mr. Eversole, she told him she was sure some boys in the class were going to blow up the lab and that she was too afraid to be there. He bartered a bargain with her that if she would just sit inside the door, he would pass her—which she says he honored with a grade of a C.

Since he was also the principal and had other duties to attend to, Mr. Eversole often came late to class, which left us to our own chemistry. Nella's fears were not as far-fetched as one might think, for our group that year did have more than its quota of mad scientists. In addition, our chemistry lab was very well stocked with a fifty-year inventory of some pretty dangerous items.

As it turned out, Nella has a permanent scar from the class—not from any explosion, but also from no thanks to me. I sharpened a few pencils for our use one day when she and I started a little horse play.

In our tug of war, a pencil slipped from her hand and

lodged just above her eye. She responded by passing out. I was much relieved when a several minutes later she again showed signs of life. A piece of the pencil lead remains in her head as a remembrance of Nella's chemistry days. She professes she is still my friend anyway. At the time, I was prepared to do one of those scaffold confessions like Granny heard from Bad Tom Smith.

Nella became one of that sizeable numbers of Witherspoon graduates who became teachers immediately on graduation. She was only seventeen years old, and her assignment was a one-room school located at Ten Mile. She was disillusioned the very first day when two young girls, ages five and six, arrived at school chewing tobacco. Nella promised them a new doll if they quit. The reward, she says, was not powerful enough; they were still chewing as the school year ended. Disheartened, Nella's teaching career lasted only one year.

Nella came to school from Gay's Creek and lived in conditions not all that different from my own had I tried to go to my own Lee County School. Her parents operated a grocery store, where every morning before she left for school she got up and made sandwiches to sell to passing workers on their way somewhere. She lived about twenty miles from Buckhorn itself and sat through a very long ride on the bus every day. In the building of the Buckhorn Dam, both her family home and their grocery store were taken by eminent domain. Her father had died just a year before, which left Nella's mother to raise eight girls alone.

Even with my "developmental problems" of being too questioning and outspoken, my junior year in school overall was a good one. School activities were plentiful. We had a club I never see in schools these days in which members joined the Civil Air Patrol. Our primary club activity was to learn to identify Soviet planes and keep a sharp eye to the skies ready to report any that we might observe flying over Buckhorn. We were convinced Witherspoon College would be a primary target of any atom bomb that might be dropped if a war started. Fortunately for us, none fell. If they had, no bunkers had been constructed for us to run to. I got my first piece of jewelry from the club—a silver lapel pin that I wore regularly in my shirt collar.

The class also put on a play, the name of which is not memorable. I do know that I was typecast by playing the role of a nerd. My older sister Joyce Ann came down special from Ohio to see the production. She was enthusiastic in her praise for my acting ability. I told her I was not really acting but just being me. I also expressed my opinion that I did have good ability for projecting volume from the stage, which is why I seemed to get so many laughs when I spoke my part. In truth, I knew the real reason the laughs came from the audience was because they saw me just being me—a nerd.

Our class was also rewarded with another outstanding English teacher that year. His instructional methods were without doubt something university professors might want to consider discussing in teacher training programs. A Quaker minister, he also gave of his time to the church. His religious convictions caused him to observe silence in almost everything he did. On the first day of school, he announced that each day when we entered the room, the directions for us would be on the board and that we were expected to follow them precisely. Those words were the absolute last he spoke for the entire semester. If students misbehaved, he simply stared them down. If they asked him a question about the assignment, he looked at them and pointed to the chalkboard. When test time came, he handed out the questions and sat silently while we wrote our answers. Most of the students grew weary with the class and made no preparation for any assignments. When he reported his grades at the end of the term, he failed just about every person in class. In contrast, I again made a good grade because I had read the book and followed the directions on the board.

The teacher only lasted one semester. Whether he left because he felt our class was not worth his time or whether school officials felt it was time for him to move on, I have never learned.

Our principal that year was new to his position, but not to Buckhorn. Edwin Keen, the son of Crit and Osha, was very well thought of in the community. He recruited his sister Jean to take over the English class. Though quiet in her demeanor, at least she did speak; and she quickly gained the respect of the students. Personally, I could hardly wait to attend her class each day, and not just for her teaching. Mrs. Wooton had such a calming disposition and a sincere interest in each and every one of us that going to her class to me was like going back to Long Shoal for some of my mother's fried potatoes and pork chops. After many years, I once asked her if she even remembered me as one of her students.

"Yes, I do remember you," she answered. I figured it must be for some awful-to-God thing I had done, but I was relieved when she added, "You always seemed to study hard and came prepared to class. I also believe you wrote a poem for class once that I thought was good enough to show to Mrs. Gabbard."

Well, that was certainly news to me. In this same conversation, I also learned that her brother's job was complicated by that very same judge of creativity, Mrs. Myrtle Gabbard, who evidently made it a habit to drop by Lafayette Hall on days she was in town to get a first-hand view of what was going on in the school. Generally, she found something she felt needed improving. Edwin became quite upset with her constant meddling. One day he stopped by his parent's home for lunch and asked his mother what landscape bush it was that grew next to the house. "Why, that's a crape myrtle," Osha told him and then asked, "Would you like a start?"

"No!" Edwin replied, "I definitely do not want a start. I want you to cut it down. I never want to be reminded of the name Myrtle again."

As the end of the year approached, everyone's attention turned to the junior-senior prom. My parents again came to my rescue by buying a suit from the Montgomery Ward catalog for me to wear. I was barely fortunate enough to get Lillian Browning (no relation that I know of) to be my date for the evening. Music was provided via phonograph records, the two of which stick in my mind being Billy Vaughan's "Melody of Love," and Ray Anthony's "Do the Hokey Pokey." Lillian and I waltzed and did whatever one would call the dance for the Hokey Pokey. I think the chronic pain I suffer these days from problems with the facet joint in my back stems from not putting my "whole body in" correctly.

Back in the dormitory, one incident highlighted the year. On a Sunday afternoon during quiet hour when no noise was tolerated at all, the building shook from the explosion of a firecracker. The building's echo acoustics only intensified the sound. Mr. Johnson had let it slip once that he kept a pistol in his apartment, so my first thought was that Mrs. Johnson had finally done him in. Instead, it was her voice that broke the total silence that followed the firecracker.

"What son of a bitch did that?" she yelled.

There was no answer then and has not been for sixty years. Quiet hour was really a quiet hour after that. We all laughed later at poor Mrs. Johnson's fall from grace. She would have justifiably laid into any one of us who used the bad words she spoke. We did not lose respect for her though, for whoever played that trick had not done her right.

Sometime during that year, a new student was welcomed to the dormitory. I only remember him by the name of Henry. He was a blonde-haired, fair-complexioned youth who was older than he appeared to be. Though diminutive in size, Henry was such a perfect physical Aryan race specimen that he could have been a poster child for Hitler's youth. The only thing we as students knew about him was that he came from Mount Sterling, which was a town out of the mountains and an unlikely place for anyone to come from to attend school at Buckhorn. Henry also had a voice that would have qualified him for the Vienna Boys' Choir. He was definitely a hit at the talent show when he sang Doris Day's "On Moonlight Bay."

Henry lived on the first floor, which meant I had little association with him. Any feelings I might have had would have been positive, but mostly he was a non-entity to me. That changed, however, when on one Saturday afternoon, I stayed back at the dormitory to listen to the broadcast of a Cincinnati Reds game. I thought everybody else had gone to a school function being held at the gym, so I welcomed the time alone to listen to the game.

I soon learned, however, that at least one other person stayed back. This I realized because the ballasts of the fluorescent lights when first turned on in our dormitory came over the air waves so loud that nothing could be heard on the radio. The sound of a jack hammer would have been more soothing to the ear. I endured this at first because I had discovered that if the lights were left on, the sound would sometimes fade off and broadcaster Wait Hoyt's voice could be heard. I was relieved when in a few minutes the sound stopped altogether, meaning the lights totally had been switched off.

This silence only lasted for a minute or so, for the lights came on again and drowned out the ball game. After a while, the pattern of sound was on-again, off-again. I decided to locate the person creating the situation. I found Henry in his room just lying on his bed. I profess with my hand on the Bible that I used the best manners I knew to explain to Henry the problem he was creating. Then I pleaded to him to either leave the lights on or off.

"Okay, I understand" was his response.

But when I returned to my room, I found the whole event repeated itself. Again, I went down and asked Henry if he could either keep the lights on or off. He again said he understood.

After a third trip, I became frustrated because it became clear to me that what was happening was intentional.

This time, I said, "Henry, I do not care if you leave the lights on or off, but what you are doing is making it impossible for me to listen to the ball game, which I feel I have the right to do."

This time, he responded with, "And I have the right to turn the lights on and off as much as I want. You can't tell me what to do."

Then out of the blue, he added, "And when Mr. Johnson gets back, I am going to tell him you called me a son of a bitch!"

Well, this last statement definitely rang my bell. I would not have used those words for anything in the world. Further, where I came from, the use of the expression meant there would be a one hundred percent chance a fight would result. I rejected his accusation and told Henry that if he did not stop, I would stop him myself.

His response was to curse me personally and to tell me, "Well, just bring it on!"

I was so angry I lost all control. I pummeled him with my fists and threw him on the floor. I then walked back to my room where I finally welcomed some peace and quiet and tuned into the Reds game without further interruption.

I also recalled advice my father gave to all of us at home. "Do your dead level best," he said, "to never get into a fight.

But if you do, leave the other person in such a condition that he will never try it again."

"Well," I thought for the first time in my life, "I guess Dad would be proud of me now!"

The problem did not end there, for I had fallen right into a trap Henry set for me. In retrospect, I am sure he had planned the whole event. As a conduct disordered person, Henry did not have to have any need or motivation for what happened; but in this case he did have a reason to further his evil scheme. He also was more than willing to take the physical beating in order for him to create more chaos, which is exactly what resulted. He may, however, have underestimated just how painful the beating ended up being.

Henry, of course, reported the event to Mr. Johnson as quickly as he could. Mr. Johnson, on hearing Henry's sad tale—practically none of which was true—called me down to the Assembly Room and made me look at Henry.

"See what you have done?" he said to me. "I guess you could not pick on someone your own size. You will apologize to him immediately."

Henry, I had to admit, was a sight. He was very green from so many bruises. His translucent skin just exaggerated the damage he had suffered. At the same time, I also recognized that nothing I might say would be heard by Mr. Johnson as a reason for my actions. Whatever the reasons were, they could not justify what I had done.

I just looked at Henry and with a heavy dose of moral equivalency, I then legally complied with Mr. Johnson's summons by saying, "Henry, I am sorry you look so bad."

In my mind, however, I felt I had not said anything about actually feeling sorry I had caused him to look that way. Mr. Johnson evidently did not pick up on my verbal maneuvering.

Instead, he followed this up by calling a special assembly where he showed off Henry as a pitiful specimen to all the boys in the dormitory. Every one there looked at me with the contempt of a child murderer. After the shock and horror of seeing one of their own so bludgeoned and mutilated, Mr. Johnson issued a final ruling to all the witnesses in the assembly meeting that no person was to speak to me until he gave them permission, which he felt might be a very long time to come. As I found my way back to my room, I heard other boys telling Henry how bad they felt for him, that they definitely would follow Mr. Johnson's directive, and that I was an outcast as far as they were concerned. Henry clearly was on a high with all the attention he received.

At the time, I had been very fortunate in getting a job cleaning one of the new buildings the school had obtained from funds from the Robinson Foundation and which served as living quarters for three teachers, two of whom included Mr. Brown and Mr. Cheek. For my work, the men paid me a total of two dollars each week. This steady income had made it possible for me to mix with others on Mr. Keen's store porch and sometimes even join those buying a snack. I also used the money to buy my first phonograph record—Eddie Fisher's "I Need You Now." Though I did not have a record player, I took the record to Aunt Georgia's house in Hazard and played it there when I was able to stay over after a ball game.

On what would have been pay day for me when I went to clean the apartment and collect my earnings, the teachers just outright told me I was fired. I was stunned and asked if my work was not acceptable. I was told my work was not the reason I was being let go. They then paid me in change and informed me that Henry would be doing their cleaning from now on. At last, I was beginning to better understand Henry's scheme.

Crest fallen, I said nothing but thanked the teachers for letting me work for them. I took their money and walked slowly back toward the dormitory. It was almost dark. As I got close to the building, at least five boys jumped from the rock wall that terraced the building. As they landed on me, my money went flying through the air. I never did have much in the way of fighting ability, but I recall kicking one in the groin, which caused him to limp off and end his part of the fight. A couple of others soon did the same. In the end, of course, I lost. Finally, they all withdrew, though I do not remember being as bruised as Henry had been. I looked for my money, but it was too dark to find it. As I went up the steps to the dormitory, I saw Mr. Johnson sitting casually at the side of the building where he had certainly seen everything that took place. He said nothing to me as I passed by him, but it was apparent that he had arranged the ambush and had actually given the signal for my attack.

I can report that no one had to look at my injuries, nor would I have consented had anyone tried. These were my wounds, and I would heal without any sympathy from anybody else. I can also report there was no special assembly where others were publically humiliated for their actions.

As it turned out, the silent treatment part of the punishment hardly fazed me. It could not carry over to the classroom, where no one in my class even heard of the problem. I was treated with the same banter from my community classmates as usual. Eventually, several dormitory boys who really felt the fight had nothing to do with them in the first place slipped and started talking to me. When they did, I just looked at them and said, "Aren't you breaking the rules?" I then walked on by with my body language telling them I had nothing to say to them.

The problem did not end there.

After a couple of weeks, I went home for a weekend visit

with my family. My granny had died at my parent's home after her one peaceful day in the whole six months she lived with them. I stayed for the funeral. Both my parents looked tired and thin, which they were because they were up with Granny night after night. While she did some sleeping the next day after her bouts, they got no sleep. They had to carry on with the farm work.

Granny's funeral was sad. She was laid out in her own home in an open casket. She was dressed in one of her best home-sewn gingham dresses with its usual heavily starched white collar. Her coffin was dignified looking; but even with the tough economic times I was used to, it looked cheap to me. The exterior of the casket appeared to be just a covering of grey felt on heavy reinforced cardboard that was sure to not last very long. The seams of the felt were already showing, and Granny had not even been put away. During the night, I visited with Granny quietly on my own, but I did not cry. Granny and I had discussed death enough for me to know that she was not there even if her body was. For the first time in my life, I grasped the full meaning of "dust to dust." I also reconciled my feelings by remembering how Granny had shed tears with me when she said she missed the presence of my grandfather.

After an all-night wake, six men carried Granny up the steep, long, and winding path up the hill to the cemetery and slowly lowered her in her casket into a wooden box that had already been placed in hand-dug grave where she rested beside my grandfather.

Granny's grave has sunk over the years, and several times we have had to fill it in with more dirt. My sister and I once sprouted the idea of replacing the sand rock headstones of Granny and Grand pap. Mother, however, strenuously objected and said, "Pap had those stones cut and engraved by Oscar Palmer. He would want them to stay right where they are."

On this visit, the conditions at home were such that I certainly never mentioned my problem at school. I probably would have been too embarrassed to do so any way.

With a sad heart, I returned to Buckhorn and silently made my way to my room. I was in shock with what I found. Literally everything I owned had been destroyed. My comb and clothes pins were broken. Even my underwear had been ripped up and thrown all over the floor. My pencils were broken, and all the pages of my notebook were torn out and wadded up. All my bed clothes had been piled in the floor. All this devastation certainly could not be the result of one of Mrs. Johnson's inspections. This was personal. And I knew right off who the person was who did the damage.

At this point, the same hostile feelings that caused me to go after Henry boiled to the surface again. It might have been all right what had happened to me. But I was not going to pass over even for a second what had happened to the things I knew my mother had worked so hard for me to have.

Life in the dormitory at Buckhorn had a darker side, a side very likely most of the boys would never want mentioned, if they even recall at all what went on. Psychologists might even describe the behavior as just a "period of adjustment." Innocence did not abound, but few were really guilty of much. But for those lacking in sexual awareness or with identity issues, the effects of what transpired were more lasting.

For me, this side of dormitory life started on the first day of school when everybody returned to the campus. There was much laughter and mixing as students scattered from room to room to see who and what was new. Though not being unfriendly, I stayed in my room because I was more interested in looking at the new books I had just purchased for school. I was drawn especially to the story by Robert Louis Stephenson which was included in full in my English book.

Suddenly one of the oldest boys in the dorm stormed into our room and struck up a conversation. "What's your name?" "Where are you from?" "How do you like Buckhorn so far?" "What work detail are you on?" These were the questions that flew back and forth, as the boy looked over my shoulder and saw my open book.

"Oh, I remember that story," he said. "It was pretty good."

Then as suddenly as he came into the room, he said he had to go to see who else was around. As he left, he yelled back at me, "Do you want to get together and do something later tonight?"

Naively, I looked up from my book and answered with something stupid like, "Sure, we can catch a parrot to ride on our shoulders and head off to Treasure Island." He laughed at my absurd answer and flew out of the room.

I never gave his question a second thought. But after all the lights went out, the boy came back to my room and climbed into my bed. What had begun as teasing ended up with touching. I had powerful and conflicted feelings. Surely this was not right, I thought. But at the same time, I did experience feelings of comfort and security.

Those feelings were in absolute contradiction to my upbringing and stirred up many family issues for me. From my father, I always felt fear and rejection even if he never intended it. A pat on my shoulder or a hug from him I can never remember.

From my older brother Jimmy, things were no better; in fact, they were worse. I am sure Jimmy had brotherly love for me because by getting out the shot gun, he temporarily stopped my father the time Dad beat me with a mop. It was after my brother left, that Dad then fired at me with the gun.

From the beginning of my life, my brother and I had a Cain and Abel existence. The day after I was born, our neighbor

Jockey Combs teasingly told Jimmy his pony was going to be given to me. It was a stupid tease. Jimmy reacted by heaving a block of coal that fortunately hit my mother's toe instead of me.

For the rest of our childhood, hardly any interaction between us ended up without some kind of a rivalry blow up. Jimmy always had to be top dog and win. He almost always was the victor in our physical fights, though I never fully conceded and found other ways to get even—like the time for retribution I pulled up some of his valuable tobacco plants.

Every time we went swimming even when he faithfully promised Mother he would not do so, Jimmy held me under the water until I was sure I was drowning. Today's news discussions of waterboarding that question its use for interrogating terrorists always reminds me of the dozen or so times I personally experienced waterboarding. The difference was that it did not happen to me to get information, for in my home I generally was out of the loop anyway. It was strictly for torture and dominance.

In a ball game, if I hit a line drive for a good hit, Jimmy always did his best to follow with a home run. If we played a game of cards, he won—even if he had to cheat. If he could not do that, he turned over the table and ended the game.

Nothing I did ever brought any lasting peace. When I was in the eighth grade my teacher Mattie Combs paid me a nickel a day for cleaning the building when the school day ended and an additional nickel a day for building fires during cold weather to get the school warmed up before everybody got there. More than once, I "loaned" this money to my brother knowing it would never be returned. That was no worry to me because I really had little opportunity to spend the money anyway. But I always thought Jimmy could at least have expressed some appreciation and for once actually mean it.

In retrospect, my brother was cursed because he better fit my father's idea of what a son should be like. He emulated my father who rewarded him for his behavior. Dad took him with him every time he went to Court Day to trade horses. The idea of throwing a "manly drunk," cursing, and standing your ground in any situation was seen as something positive. Everybody knew Jimmy as "Rouster Browning's boy," which in itself gave him status.

Unfortunately, when Jimmy had his own family later in life, he developed the same behavior patterns as my father. He drank until he got out of control, and he terrorized his own family. Later in his thirty's in strict violation of his parole from a prison sentence for shooting someone in the leg in a bar room brawl, he started carrying around in his vehicle the same sixteen gauge shot gun he had drawn on my father. By now, to make the weapon even more deadly, he had sawed off the barrel. He thought he had killed a woman with whom he had an affair when he blew off the wig she was wearing. Thinking the worst, he ended it all when he then aimed the gun at his own head and blew out his brains. My mother's brother, Uncle Jim, helped remove some of his remains from a tree near where the shooting took place.

This experience with the older boy, though not rejected, was in direct conflict with my upbringing, which in many ways was more than Puritanical. There was never any acknowledgement of anything during the day, but he came to my room several times after that. One evening, later in the year, while the boy was in my room, the sound of Mr. Johnson's cane pounded down the hall. I told the boy he had to leave, but he whispered to me not to worry. Mr. Johnson did not pass by my room. Instead, he barged in and flipped on the light switch.

I was so scared and ashamed that I ran right by Mr. Johnson and up to the attic which was used to store hundreds of army bunk mattresses. I wormed my way among the stacks and hid out. Mr. Johnson had many boys looking for me for hours, but I was never discovered.

The next day, however, while other boys were away completing their farm chores and I was taking my afternoon nap as per my individual work shift schedule, Mr. Johnson's cane came thumping down the hall to my room again. This time there was no escape. I expected the worst. Instead, he sat down by my bed and told me that I had nothing of which to be afraid or of which to be ashamed. He touched me orally. When he left the room, I went straight to the bath room, vomited, and took the longest shower of my life.

It seems Mr. Johnson's "discovery" of the boy and I had not been a surprise, though my reaction was. My reaction also made it clear to Mr. Johnson that I would never be one of his group even as a joke, which I am sure it must have been to others. He never spoke of it again, nor did I. I do remember comments from him on other occasions to be more than gross, when he would say something like "For this job, I want a boy with hair under his arm pits" (or in some other location).

The boy did not come to my room anymore. He has since passed away, and I have heard he was a faithful husband and a good father.

While I certainly did not recall any of these events in any sequence or with any rational reasoning, seeing the destruction of my belongings brought forth a tsunami of unresolved and repressed feelings. I would not let this pass. This time I marched down to Mr. Johnson's apartment and demanded that he come up to my room.

Walking slowly and with his cane thumping on the floor, Mr. Johnson followed me up to my room without any comment at all except for a stern "What is your problem?" He needed no answer, for his face blanched when he saw my room.

I spoke with low volume but with no quiver in my voice as I stated, "Mr. Johnson, this has gone far enough. I have not done anything to deserve this. You not only let this stuff take place, you have actually set it up. You know that I know enough to cause a lot of trouble around here. Unless this stops and things are made right, the whole world is going to hear from me!"

Suddenly all the macho commentary that I had become accustomed to hearing from Mr. Johnson was not there anymore. He was totally drained of any color. As I looked at him, I saw that he was not just a physical cripple but was crippled in a lot more ways than that. Instead of anger, my feelings for just a second turned to sympathy; and I felt sorry that I made my threat. Making threats was not my style, for I had by this time kept my feelings and my secret for over two years. Up to this point, everything that I experienced I felt had been my own doing with no blame for anybody else.

Mr. Johnson's only response was "I do not know what has happened here, Alex, but I will make things right."

He neither admitted his actions had led to this scene nor that he was sorry about it. But he clearly did not want any public airing. Even today I doubt he did know what had occurred, but I am also confident he had just as good an idea of who had destroyed my things as I did.

Mr. Johnson turned and feebly went back downstairs.

Meanwhile, I just sat on the side of my bed and hung my head and closed my eyes tight. My feelings were of total hopelessness.

My feelings turned to dread and then to relief when sometime later, Mr. Johnson returned. On entering the room, he pulled out fifteen dollars, which he offered to me.

"I hope this will replace your things," said. Then he added, "But if it does not, I will give you whatever else it takes."

I said nothing, not even thanks. The next day I went to

Mr. Keen's store and replaced my laundry supplies and other personal items. It was never mentioned in any assembly, but shortly afterward the word got around that it was acceptable to talk to Alex again.

When most people talk about the fires at Buckhorn in the 50's, they only refer to the destruction of Worthington Hall, Englis Hall, McKenzie Refectory, and Faith Hall. There was a third fire on the campus that many people do not remember at all. A log building back up the hill from our dormitory was visible from its high perch on the mountain. While at Buckhorn, I did not know its name or original purpose. But I have since learned the building was known as the Gabbard House. When Dr. Gabbard graduated from seminary in 1916, he returned to Buckhorn to serve for six years as assistant minister at the church. The building was constructed for his living quarters. Over the years, the building continued to house individuals who served in administrative capacities for the school. I believe that during the years I was at Buckhorn, Edwin Keen and his family may have lived there while he was principal of the school. After he left his position, the building sat empty. All of us had been directed to never venture up the hill to the building, and we all complied except for one student. One day the building burst into flames and was quickly destroyed.

Shortly after that, Henry just disappeared from the campus. We all wondered what happened to him, though personally I did not care. Later I heard that he lost his job cleaning for the teachers because things there went missing. After that, we then heard a rumor that he had been sent back to Mount Sterling because he had started the fire. We also heard he came to Buckhorn in the first place as a diversion from being sent to juvenile reform school for stealing from a jewelry store. I cannot vouch personally if any of the rumors were true. I just know he left the school in a hurry.

Though I eventually regained my status in the dormitory, no one ever bothered to ask my side of the Henry escapade. It did not make any difference. I kept my own silence—for good reason. From then on, both of the Johnsons treated me with full respect as I took my place in the social order expected from older students in the dormitory. Mrs. Johnson and I became winning partners when we played Rook.

CHAPTER 11

Angles, Trapezoids, and a Tumultuous Twelfth

My geometry class paid almost immediate dividends for me. When I left campus for the month or so I was not obligated to work on the school farm at the end of my junior year, my father shared with me that he had learned the government farm office for Lee County was looking for people to measure tobacco bases. The pay would be great, six dollars for each base. To get the job, applicants passed a math test and completed a training program on government regulations. For a high school student to be hired was about as likely as being kicked by a three-legged mule. Perhaps I had more gall than brains, but I immediately told my father I wanted to go for the job.

Dad was also a person willing to take chances. He drove me to Beattyville. When I entered the agriculture offices and announced my intentions, the staff wanted to know if perhaps I was confused. I assured them I was not and completed the application. When other applicants showed up—all ranging from thirty to forty years in age and some who had done the work before—many asked me if I was crazy and did I know what I was getting myself into. Even the test proctor looked at me suspiciously.

Their looks and comments did have merit. Measuring

tobacco bases in the 50's not only required math skills, it was somewhat dangerous. In those days, the government controlled the production of tobacco by granting acreage allotments. (Today tobacco production is controlled differently. A farmer can market a specified number of pounds, and the government is not concerned with how much land is required for growing the tobacco.) In the 50's, farmers could market as much tobacco as they could grow but only on the amount of land the government allowed them on which to grow it. Any tobacco marketed on land not allotted had to be sold on a "red card" at the annual auctions, meaning the buyers could offer about what they wanted to for the crop. On a red card, the price was always so low the farmers spent more money growing the product than what they got paid for it.

If the measurement of the farmer's base came out to be more than the government allotted, the farmer had the option of cutting down the excess area or selling the crop without price support. Farmers came up with all sorts of ways to get as much tobacco from the land included in the base allotment as possible. Some went so far as to plant fields hidden away on their farms which they never reported to the agent doing the measurement. A more common effort was to plant the acreage in such a way as to make it virtually impossible to plot and measure. A few farmers actually tried to intimidate the agent into reporting false measures. Some growers could become vicious if they thought the person doing the measuring was going to report acreage that would cause plants to have to be chopped down or cause them to market their year's work on a red card.

To protect the integrity of the measurements, spot checkers randomly visited farms to do a second measurement. If that person's figures did not consistently agree with the first measurement, the person who turned in the original figures was let go immediately. The government also flew airplanes over farms to try to catch farmers who had hidden fields. The allotment process had gotten so precise that if a farmer's crop one year had a very large amount of pounds sold, he could be pretty sure his base would be measured twice the next year.

I was fortunate to pass the test because I had learned the formulas in our geometry class for figuring the areas of circles, squares, triangles, and trapezoids. Despite my age, I was hired because of my test scores. But I soon learned that my knowledge of geometry provided only the rudimentary skills necessary for the job. The base also had to be plotted out on paper to show how and where the measurements were taken. Many farmers, including my own father, contrived plans to make this step as hard as possible. Bases up our way were always planted along the creeks that meandered first to the right and then to the left, so the agent found it difficult to draw the plot. This did not end the difficulty. The farmer then had to hold one end of a chain while the agent walked to the area drawn on the plot and recorded the distance. Many farmers developed palsy the minute they were handed the chain.

Many if not most wanted to know the outcome immediately of the measurement and typically commented that they would rather cut down any excess right then rather than have any overage reported. Agents were told directly this was not allowed. Certainly, if some of the people I knew had learned such information, very few really would have wanted to actually cut down even one plant. Instead, there would likely have been a quick argument, if not a fight. Had that happened, a just-turned-sixteen-year-old kid would not have much of a fighting chance.

The job also required a great deal of walking, as that was generally the means of getting from one base to another. Going up hollers and meeting people I had never seen was a test in itself. Anyone from the government was not likely to be welcomed at all and most assuredly would not be invited for bite to eat. A person my age in a position to affect an older person's livelihood naturally was treated with a great deal of suspicion. I had one thing going for me. My father was pretty well known throughout the county for his knowledge of horses and mules. Many people had traded animals with him, and others had thrown a drunk or two with him. When I introduced myself as Rouster Browning's boy, most everybody dropped their guard. Some even said, "That's good, boy, I know you will treat me fair."

Such comments always startled me because my father also had quite a reputation for being a shrewd horse trader. I learned from him the secret to a good trade was one in which both sides felt they had received a good deal. Dad evidently had skill for making the people he traded with think they had gotten the best mule or horse ever reared. Sometimes he returned from Court Day with as much as $30 and the same animals he left home with. How, I questioned could everybody still feel they got a good deal that day?

My month of work went by without much difficulty. The spotters verified my work and found no problems. I never heard anything from anybody directly, but some people in the Beattyville office made positive comments about my work to my father. For the first time, I could see in his face that he was proud of me. He alerted me ahead of time to a couple of people he was sure would either try to force me to report false data or likely would not tell me all of the land they really had in tobacco. He was right. One got caught and had to market his entire crop on a red card. My father's knowledge of people in our area was so deep he would have made a good candidate for sheriff. For sure, he knew where all the moon shine stills were and of all the people who sold illegal alcohol. He could have cleaned up the whole county for a year or so armed with that knowledge.

Tobacco was about the only cash crop people had up our way. My dad always tried to grow the biggest plants possible and to get the tobacco to market in time for Christmas. Our allotment of six tenths of an acre in a good year would sometimes bring in as much as $1,500. This was the money that would get us through the whole next year, so it was important to get as much of the proceeds into the bank as possible.

Three things were exceptions and bought immediately. Dad was insistent that we get fresh fruit for Christmas. When he returned from the tobacco market, we all ran out to meet him; for we knew he would come back with apples, oranges, bananas, and nuts. Mom always used these ingredients in her Christmas Jell-O which she placed in covered bowls stored in hens' nests in which she made use of the seasonally cold weather to set the Jell-O.

Dad also came home with a battery for our radio. After months of not being able to listen to the Grand Ole Opry, the sounds of Cousin Minnie Pearl's jokes about trying to find a feller, Hank Williams' "Lovesick Blues," Hank Snow's train songs, and my favorite, Roy Acuff's "Great Speckled Bird" all lifted our spirits for the holidays.

Unfortunately, it was also a pretty sure thing that Dad would come home lit. Sometimes, his moods were good, and my younger sister Mary would sit with him and sing all night long. She was pretty good. Dad, on the other hand, was mostly just loud. The sound of a drunk singing all night was painful to everybody's ears except his. For each drunk, we prayed it would be a singing drunk and not a crying drunk. If I heard things drifting toward the latter and heading off into demons and devils, sometimes I slipped out of bed and went to Granny's. But even when his moods turned sour, Mary often had the skill to guide my father through the night peacefully. Whatever the Christmas season turned out to be, it was always the time our family most eagerly waited for and also the time we most dreaded.

That was how our own yearly tobacco growing ended, with fresh fruit, a battery for the radio, and a drunk by my father. But for this particular season (June and July) during the time I had at home from school, I earned money to help pay my tuition for my final year at Buckhorn. There was even some to give back to my family. This made me the proudest I think I ever have been.

There was another event that summer that was not so pleasant. I had to face the reality that I no longer could hang on to my best friend, my horse Jim. Dad in a moment he certainly regretted had given Jim to me as a colt. It must have been a weak moment for him because he knew I did not part with my animal friends. Dad got Jim as throw-in when he traded for the colt's mother. The sorrel colt already knew tricks when Dad brought him home. If you put your hand under his chin, he would rear up on cue.

Jim was not a horse to be used for plowing. In fact, I was about the only person who could get him to work at all. Jim was part race horse, built for speed, which he demonstrated every time my cousin Henry Glen came to visit and tried to ride him. Jim never even objected when sister Mary and I rode him double. With others, he was prone to rearing up in an effort to throw them or to run away so fast as to cause them to fall out of the saddle.

Because Jim was not a work animal, keeping him over during the winter meant corn and hay would have to be used for him and not for the other animals that helped us survive. My father broached the subject and tried to persuade me to trade Jim for a cow, no doubt thinking my great success on the morning milk crew would be a motivation for me to make the trade. I listened to the terms, and I knew what had to be done. I went to the barn and talked with Jim for hours. I told Jim that if Black Beauty could endure all the things that occurred in the book, I knew he could because he was better than Black Beauty to me. Jim only attended to the sounds of my voice, of course, but he perked up his ears, listened intently, and stood at attention until I was finished. I hugged him, returned home, and told Dad I would make the trade. I knew my father would not keep him for even a month after I left home that summer. I returned to Buckhorn knowing that I would never see Jim again. I later heard stories about Jim's good fortunes, but I knew they were all lies told to me to try to give me some assurance that I had done the right thing in making the trade for the cow, whose name I do not even recall. She would never be my friend; Jim always would be.

My senior year at Buckhorn began and continued for several weeks with little change in my routine. Sometime previously during my stay at Buckhorn, my mother had managed to save enough money to buy me an Airline radio from Montgomery Ward. I listened to music every time I could. Especially at night I delighted in picking up far away stations. Randy's Record Shop from Gallatin, Tennessee, seemed to have all the music that later became known as rhythm and blues. With its frequent ads for Royal Palm hair dressing for which I had no use and packages of records for sale, the program was broadcast on WLAC in Nashville. The powerful station WWL in New Orleans was the station to dial in if the choice of music was the blues. This music was not the country music we listened to at home, but I loved it.

Many people are so affected by historical events, such as the assassination of President Kennedy or the terrorist attack on the World Trade Center, they can tell you exactly where they were and what they were doing when the event occurred. In my case, I can tell you exactly where I was the first time I heard the Platters' song, "Only You." The Airline radio was definitely my best friend for all the time I had it at Buckhorn.

The radio almost got me in trouble though. I slept with it close to my ear so no one could hear it, but sometimes I overlooked the fact that the radio had a dial light. Mrs. Johnson, walking around the building at night, could see the glow. She did not yell at me. But she always said, "Alex, turn off your radio." I did until I heard her come back into the building. Then I turned the radio on again and covered it and myself with my blanket so the room stayed dark—just in case she made another round. The dial light I later learned was wired into the electrical components of the radio. When it burned out, the radio stopped working altogether. That happened during the early weeks of my senior year. In the space of just a few months I lost my horse and my radio. Times were not good.

Since I knew this was my last year of high school, I quickly began the process of looking into where I might go to college. As my fortunes had changed very little, I knew the school had to be inexpensive. My research led me to Pikeville College, a Presbyterian school in the very eastern tip of the state of Kentucky. I learned students could earn their room and board by working in the cafeteria. Three hours of work each day would pay for room and three meals.

Even more intriguing, the college catalog said students could be admitted to college if they had 15½ credits on their transcripts. That seemed not right to me because in those days it took 16 credits to earn a high school diploma. I wrote the school and found the requirement was not a misprint. When I looked at my record, I found that if I passed all my classes I would have exactly 15½ credits at the end of the first semester.

Armed with this news, I wrote to Mr. McClure and told him what I had learned. He volunteered to drive me to Pikeville to see the college. As we drove through the college campus, I idly commented that the building we were passing was the girls' dormitory. He stumped me by asking how I knew that. I did not have an answer. But I was right. Mr. McClure looked at me as if I were psychic. He already had a much higher opinion of me than I deserved, but this one little thing made him a firm believer that one from his flocks from Long Shoal was a miracle kid—more fantastic thinking on his part.

While visiting the school, Mr. McClure introduced me to Dr. Paige, the president of Pikeville College. Dr. Paige happened to mention that the college offered full tuition scholarships to valedictorians of their class. Reverend McClure assured Dr. Paige that I would be eligible for the scholarship. I knew I had a good academic record but had no idea what my class standing was. I thought Reverend McClure was engaging in even more of his far out thinking for which he had absolutely no facts to back him up. It was right, however, that the scholarship, if attainable, would just about fulfill the dream I had of attending college. With both work opportunity and paid tuition, college financing might just be possible. The only real money I would have to come up with would be for my clothes, books, and supplies. (I later sold my cow for $100, which I had traded my horse Jim for, and went to Rose Brothers Bargain Store in Beattyville to purchase those items when I ventured off to Pikeville to begin college in January, 1956.)

When we returned to Buckhorn, I asked our new principal that year, Mr. Colwell, what my class rank was. He determined it was the highest in the class. I then asked him if he would verify to Pikeville that I was the valedictorian of the class.

"I do not think I can do that, Alex," he said, "for you have not met our graduation requirements of sixteen credits." On a technicality he was definitely correct. I reported the bad news to Mr. McClure, who unknown to me then made a visit to meet with the principal. After the meeting, Mr. McClure contacted me and informed me that Mr. Colwell had decided he could after all write a letter verifying my honor to Pikeville.

Fifty years after my exit from Buckhorn, classmate Creta Rose Gay came up to me and while laughing told me how glad she had been when I left the campus.

"Why would you say that, Creta?" I asked her. "I always thought you and I were friends while we were in school."

"Oh, we were and are," she responded. "But when you left, I moved up in my class standing and was named valedictorian of the class."

"Well, that's great!" I told her. "I am sure you deserved it." I sincerely meant what I said, for never that I remember did I ever see myself in competition with others for grades while I was in school. Grades always meant everything to me but only as a measure of what opinion I thought my teachers had of my work, not whether my work was better than that of anybody else.

I learned that not only Creta had been named valedictorian. Two students, Patsy Combs and Pauline Colwell, the daughter of the principal, were named co-salutatorians. My departure evidently enriched the standing of several students. I certainly did not miss any of the fanfare of graduation's honors. I was just happy for the letter the principal wrote to enable me to get the $65 per semester credit for my tuition. After all the decades that have passed, I also remain very grateful for all the lobbying efforts of the good Reverend McClure.

Though my entrance to college was settled, things were not quite over for me at Buckhorn. No, I first had to survive yet another encounter with Mrs. Alta Wooton. In all her wisdom, she came up with yet another rule variation for procedures for us to follow in the dining hall. We all just looked at each other one day, when she announced that all students would remain at their tables until everyone had completed their meals, as had been the long tradition at Witherspoon.

This throw-back rule was missing a little logic. In the days the tradition was started, all students sat down at their tables at the same time; so it was reasonable they would all leave at the same time. The current procedure, however, was that we arrived at our tables after going through the cafeteria line. One could be well into dessert when a new group might just be getting through the line.

Just three weeks before I was to leave campus, I faced this exact dilemma. I went through line and sat at my table where I dined alone. When I was almost finished, three or four other students seated themselves there. They came as a group and engaged themselves in continued conversation from when they entered the building. What their topic was I do not recall, but it did not involve me. In fact, it would have been rude of me to try to inject myself into their conversation. But I knew the rule. I could not excuse myself until they finished eating. I felt somewhat like a hostage. My relief came from the table next to ours when others there and I began talking with each other. I did not leave our table, but I did move my chair somewhat and talked with these friends.

Suddenly from behind, I felt myself in motion. With rocket force, Mrs. Wooton shoved me under my table so hard my rib cage hurt from my bombardment with the table at which I was now sitting. She reminded me in very angry terms that I was not permitted to talk with anyone other than those at my own table, a fine point she had not mentioned when she instituted her latest law. I was embarrassed and also angry with her for what she had done. Would it have been such difficulty I thought for her to ask me to move closer to my table group? I held my tongue and said nothing. I simply got up from the table and took my plate, glass, knife, and fork up to the counter and left the building. As I departed, Mrs. Wooton followed me to the door and told me I could not come back to the dining hall until I apologized for my behavior and until I was willing to follow the rules.

I then did open my mouth. "I will starve to death before I apologize to you," I said. "If anybody should apologize, it should be you. I am a human being, not an animal. And I deserve respect as much as you do."

Mrs. Wooton was not in the mood nor accustomed to having anyone answer her when she issued an order. She immediately reported my behavior to Mrs. Johnson, who patiently listened to her complaints about me. Instead of getting on my case, Mrs. Johnson asked me what had happened. When I gave her my story, for some reason, she also patiently listened to me.

I was shocked to hear her say she believed me. She told me that in spite of my feelings, however, I needed to make things right with Mrs. Wooton. "Otherwise, you will not be able to eat in the dining hall anymore." "Alex, there is nothing else I can do about it," she added.

I told Mrs. Johnson I would rather eat peanut butter and crackers for the last weeks I would be at Buckhorn rather than apologize.

I was amazed when she said after she spent a long time thinking about my comment, "Well, I guess that would be possible."

Having food in the dormitory was not permitted, but evidently Mrs. Johnson was willing to let me forgo the rules. She also told me that if I wanted to keep some milk in her own refrigerator she would let me do that.

That is what I did for the last three weeks I was at Buckhorn. I ate peanut butter and crackers and potted meat. Using my new diet plan, my high school education came to a halt at the end of the semester on December 23, 1955—"not with a bang, but a whimper." There were no ceremonies and there was no celebration. There were not even very many good-byes. I left the way I came in, with my suitcase—except for a quick hug and a "best wishes" from of all people, Rhoda Johnson.

Whatever chance the Society of Soul Winners hoped to achieve with me ended on that day. I am not ready to report on my soul's future. But I am ready to report that I know which side of the plate both forks go, that I do not shake out my napkin like a towel before placing in on my lap, and that I try to not talk when my mouth is full. In this regard, Witherspoon College was a success.

I figured no one had minded my departure until many years later when I ran into my friend Nella Johnson. She told me she was quite lost when I just disappeared. I was touched, and I asked her why. "Well," she said, "you always had your homework or your notes and you let me copy from them when I got to school every day."

"Which class was that for?" I asked.

"All of them," she replied.

My peace with Buckhorn was made two years later. I had done well in public speaking at Pikeville, and Dr. Paige had contacted churches throughout Eastern Kentucky to let them know the college could arrange a guest speaker for any Sunday the regular pastor had to be away. The churches were, of course, to make a donation to the college for this service. The college dressed me up in a new suit, shirt, tie, and shoes and sent me out as the school's representative. I memorized entirely word for word a fifteen-minute sermon. There were many calls. Thirty-one times when I was a sophomore in college I visited practically every Presbyterian Church around.

On one of those dates I was the guest speaker at the Maysville Presbyterian Church where I finally got to meet Miss Mary Wilson, the angel lady who arranged to send Christmas gifts to us on Long Shoal. During the service, I gave her a public thanks for everything she had sent to me over the years. When the service was over, someone from the church whispered to me something that was hard for me to believe.

Miss Mary had nothing herself to send, and she was as poor as the proverbial church mouse. Evidently her condition had done nothing to keep her from asking for others—especially for me.

Another of my stops was Buckhorn. My family was so proud of my notoriety that Uncle Henry came in from Newport, Kentucky and brought mother to Buckhorn to hear me speak that day. I believe that was the only time she ever visited the campus while I attended.

This time as I spoke from the pulpit, I was not typecast as a nerd. I recited all my lines I had committed to memory, and I spoke with my clearest and loudest voice. I did ponder what I would do if someone dropped something while I was speaking. Fortunately, no one did. There was a pretty good turn-out to hear one of their own by the good people of Buckhorn.

As was the custom begun by Harvey Murdoch, I went out front at the end of the service to shake hands individually with each person who attended church that day. As Mrs. Alta Wooton emerged from the group, I grew a little tense. We looked at each other a little hesitantly. I spoke first. "Mrs. Wooton," I said, "I am sorry for all the grief I caused you."

"That is all right, Alex," she said. "I am sorry also. And you gave a good talk today."

Though I do not have a graduation diploma from Buckhorn, I have two things worth more than any piece of paper and a rare something I am sure most dormitory boys wish they had: a hug from Rhoda Johnson and a compliment from Alta Wooton.

. . . .

Many years later, I was in conversation with someone about my experiences at Buckhorn. The person saddened me by saying, "You know after Rhoda Johnson died, Scott Johnson took his pistol and killed himself."

Afterword—Erosion

The Appalachian Mountains are geologically unique. Instead of being formed by volcanic action by typical plate movement, they were created from the crunch of two sections of the African continent that broke off, floated away, and slammed into the coast of North America. The uplift must have been something to see. From this collision, the mountains rose to heights taller than Mount Everest. Also, from this collision, the mountains developed like folds of corrugated paper—except the Appalachians do not run very much in ranges. They are tricky. Just when a person thinks he will traverse along a certain valley, he will suddenly confront another mountain that sits squarely in a different direction of the valley he is traveling. Exposed rocks sometimes run in vertical layers, instead of horizontal. It is easy to get lost in the Appalachians, both literally and figuratively.

By now, through eons of time, erosion has reduced the height of the mountains to the point that Mount Mitchell in North Carolina is the tallest peak in the range at only 6,683 feet. Whatever evolves for future civilization in the Appalachian Mountains, rest assured in the end Nature will dictate the final result. It likely will do so through erosion. Erosion does not just wear away soil from the mountains; it wears away the very souls of people who live there. When the builders of Witherspoon College developed the log campus, they just borrowed the virgin trees from the mountains and shaped them into edifices where they could work to complete their mission of providing for the education and moral development of people they felt were in need of such. In the case of Witherspoon College, at least in a physical sense, Nature has taken back what the builders borrowed.

Having studied the history of the institution and reflecting on my own time there, I now better understand this process of erosion, at least as the term might be used as a metaphor. Originally, the intent of the Society of Soul Winners was to promote individual salvation rather than social change. However, through their work, the purpose was expanded to do just that—make changes in the social order of the people the Soul Winners served. Evidently the Soul Winners felt it necessary to change those of us native to the mountains from being "other," meaning different, and "unchurched," in order to accomplish their primary goal: lead us to salvation. ("Other" and "unchurched" were Guerrant's terms and crop up frequently in scholarly works involving the mountains.) The Society of Soul Winners dissolved in the 20's. But a collateral effect of their work—to provide education for people who had little to no educational opportunity—continued long after the Soul Winners were no more. In the Kentucky Mountains, one of those "settlement" schools was Witherspoon College. In the 50's, that mission also ended.

Since that happened, the work has evolved into the Buckhorn Children and Family Service, whose stated mission today is to provide "compassionate and dignified residential care and treatment of troubled youth," provide "treatment foster care and adoption services," and if necessary, provide "residential services." Sometimes erosion does not outright eliminate, but the process does always make changes.

Those changes as of today mean that Buckhorn operations are no longer confined to just one location. Instead, multi-counties and even multi-states benefit from the program of services. Now, in addition to physical care, "clinical teams" are at work, including such specialties as psychiatry, professionally trained counselors, direct care staff, nursing, dietician, and school and community partners. Just one person from the actual community of Buckhorn is listed on the current Board of Directors. And just one link is made to the Buckhorn Lake Presbyterian Church. That is correct. In reviewing the most recent information on the program, I only found the word Presbyterian mentioned once.

I certainly mean no disrespect for the good work going on by this organization, for it unquestionably is sorely needed. However, I have a hard time to keep from grinning when I see the word "dietician" listed as a staffing position and at the same time recall poor Mrs. Wooton and the meals she and her girls served up to us at Buckhorn when I was there. I am confident I will pay a penalty if there is such a thing as an after-life for all the indigestion I caused Mrs. Wooton. But if I end up in God's Court, I will defend myself by stating that in my case Mrs. Wooton caused me a lot of indigestion herself. In addition to the dangerous milk, burnt biscuits, and treacle, other menu items often consisted of government surplus "pickled" butter, soup beans with rocks not sorted out, and hard cheese—also government surplus and the tastiest item of the group. The best I can say as a culinary review of the food is that I never remember going hungry while I was in school.

The log college envisioned by the Society of Soul Winners, Harvey Murdoch, and all the benefactors from Brooklyn, New York exists no more. The settlement school that transformed from these early developers was on its last legs when I departed and exists no more. Every year there are fewer and fewer of us who lived the campus life of Buckhorn; and in just a few short years, there will be none of us. We are in many ways like the great American chestnut tree—in our cases, smitten by the blight of life. Erosion does have its consequences.

A search of the literature having to do with Witherspoon

209

College these days will likely result in great detail coming from professors from the halls of ivy. For example, The Wilson Library at the University of North Carolina at Chapel Hill has set aside eight linear feet of shelf space just for its collection titled Edward O. Guerrant Papers, 1856-1917. (For this, blame Guerrant, not the university. His diary itself consists of twelve times as many words as the book you hold.) Other references are made to Witherspoon College or the Soul Winners in such erudite publications as *Appalachian Mountain Religion: A History* by Deborah Vansau McCauley; *Appalachia on Our Mind* by Henry D. Shapiro; and *Eastern Kentucky and the Civil War* by Marlitta H. Perkins. The list goes on.

No disrespect is meant to these intellects and their writings, but after reading what they have set forth, the term intellectual erosion comes to mind. Analysis and generalizations are for historians and sociologists. I have no big interest to involve myself on any controversy related to "mountain religion" versus church denominational competition and imposition of values. I have even less energy to react to stereotypes which cause people from our area to be referred to as poor "mountain whites," though I do enjoy hearing the objection to the term voiced by a North Carolina school superintendent because he thought it made us sound like a new rose that had just come on the market. I do read with great interest any publications in which I find references to either of my own ancestors' struggles during the Civil War because in many ways I do not feel their causes have yet been settled in my country. These scholars are to be commended for their work, and all that I have read does appear to have sound theses.

Because mine is primarily a personal story, I recognize that it occupies only a small niche in the topics referenced above. However, before erosion on a personal level is complete, I have tried to fill in a few blanks on the efforts of some wonderful and caring people who founded, supported, and delivered services to those of us who benefited from Witherspoon College, as well as to report on what it was like to be on the receiving end of those services. Others may have a different story to tell in that regard. I leave to them that job—if they feel my story is not accurate or creates a false impression.

I believe the Soul Winners had some success as far as my own life is concerned. As evidence, after I left Buckhorn, I attended Pikeville College for three years and then received my undergraduate degree from Morehead State University. I later received a graduate degree from that university as a school guidance counselor. After this, I completed post-graduate work at The Ohio State University in psychology. I took additional course work at Miami University in Ohio and at Xavier University, where one of my professors was a Jesuit priest. I also completed post-graduate work in school administration at Wright State University. And through a fellowship from *The Wall Street Journal*, I have even had some training in journalism at The University of Oregon.

I am also happy to report that my grades were good at all of the afore-mentioned universities, including the best grade point average in my class at Pikeville when I transferred to Morehead State. I mention this not to be a braggart, but to point out that some poor soul from the head of a holler on Long Shoal did have a little bit of a brain and a deep desire to learn. The Soul Winners provided a means for this desire to be met. On the side of Nature, my genes to support learning came at least in part from a Union soldier. On the side of Nurturance, work from a damned Confederate is to be thanked. In the matter of politics, I deny any influence from Nature or Nurturance from Andrew Jackson or his Democrat off-spring.

Thankfully, I did not answer a call to become a Presbyterian minister. Instead, I spent forty-three years as an educator. Four of those years, unfortunately, might be considered a failure—at least in terms of accomplishing many of the goals of the Soul Winners. During that four-year period, I became just the third school superintendent of the twentieth century for the Breathitt County Schools when I worked there in the late 80's. While I was there, one of our schools, Highland Elementary, burned— deliberately. This structure was one of the last remaining buildings of another settlement school that came from E. O. Guerrant's work. A principal at one of the county schools, who I should have fired for not taking care of his school very well, later, through politics, became superintendent for the system. He is now facing prison time for vote buying, and the whole governance of the county's educational program has been taken over by the State of Kentucky. Erosion appears to be very active in Breathitt County.

There are two remaining points I wish to make in concluding this book. One has to do with moral development. Certainly many incidents recorded in these pages have dealt with this concern. In my studies of morality, I have concluded that moral development has best been explored by Lawrence Kohlberg, ranked as the sixteenth most influential psychologist. Ultimately, according to Kohlberg, the highest level of moral development is one in which a person takes action based on the principles of justice. If justice guided our actions, there would be little need for rules or laws because we would make our decisions based on what is right and not on what we are required to do. For example, a person would not speed on the highway for fear of a ticket from an officer of the law. Instead, the person would drive safely for the benefit of others and there would be no need for posted speed limits at all. Kohlberg did conclude, however, that he never was able to identify even one human being who consistently operated at this highest level.

My reason for referring to this concept is that I believe that all the good people (students and school authorities) at

Buckhorn were driven to at the very least move in the direction of this highest level, even with the character flaws relayed in these writings. Well, perhaps there was one exception. I cannot quite accept even now that Henry had much of a conscience at all. I do wonder sometimes whatever became of him, just in an academic way.

My final point has reference to Erik Erikson's "Eight Stages of Man." The last of these stages we face in old age, which for the sake of Erikson's theory occurs somewhere between age 65 and death. At my age, I cannot deny my place on his chart. The dilemma we all face at this stage is one of *integrity* versus *despair*. If we feel we have accomplished something with our lives, then we now see ourselves as worthwhile human beings; and if we have developed a sense of personal integrity, then we can withstand the physical disintegration that is sure to follow. The resolution of this social and age dilemma leads to that wonderful thing called wisdom. I leave it to the reader to judge whether any of these pages is a record of a little bit of wisdom or that of a half-wit.

Without doubt, some people who attended Witherspoon may protest my writing these pages, and especially including events they feel would better be left alone. I protest. I would have no personal integrity if I skipped these details. My intent has definitely not been to portray myself as a victim. *I was not a victim.* On the other hand, institutions survive only in history books by out-shining any mistakes that may have been committed by any one or even a group of individuals.

If Witherspoon College is thought of at all, the word that should come first to attention is gratitude. Where would those of us be who lived on the campus of Buckhorn had Witherspoon College not been there? I dare say we are all better for what happened to us at Buckhorn; even with the grinding erosion of the living together we endured.

CPSIA information can be obtained at www.ICGtesting.com
Printed in the USA
BVOW071416250613

324258BV00001B/2/P